The

Emotional

Calendar

The
Emotional
Calendar

Understanding Seasonal Influences and
Milestones to Become Happier,
More Fulfilled, and in
Control of Your Life

John R. Sharp, M.D.

St. Martin's Griffin
New York

The Library of Congress has cataloged the Henry Holt edition as follows:

Sharp, John R., M.D.
The emotional calendar : understanding seasonal influences and milestones to become happier, more fulfilled, and in control of your life / John R. Sharp.—1st ed.
p. cm.
Includes bibliographical references and index.
ISBN 978-0-8050-9130-4
1. Emotions. 2. Self-realization. 3. Self-control. I. Title.
BF511.S513 2011
155.9—dc22   2010024892

ISBN 978-1-250-00262-4 (trade paperback)

Originally published in hardcover format by Times Books, an imprint of Henry Holt and Company

First St. Martin's Griffin Edition: January 2012

10 9 8 7 6 5 4 3 2 1

*For Ezra and Max**

*My late grandfather, Dr. Ezra A. Sharp,
and my late great-uncle, Rabbi Israel M. Goldman,
whose lives provided inspiration and wise counsel
throughout all of the seasons

Contents

PART III 🔲 EMOTIONAL HOTSPOTS: IT'S THAT TIME OF YEAR AGAIN

PART IV 🐉 AWARENESS

Author's Note

This book covers a lot of ground, incorporating material from neuroscience and psychoanalysis, meteorology and earth sciences, as well as anthropology and sociology. I am a psychiatrist and neuropsychiatrist (which means that, unlike psychologists, I am also a medical doctor), so my areas of expertise are in psychiatry, psychopharmacology, brain science, and general medicine. I confess that I am not a meteorologist or a sociologist. Nor am I an expert on geophysics or on the seasonal or cultural differences we find around the world.

I am fortunate, therefore, to have worked with a very talented team of researchers and editors in the creation of this book. They helped me gather information on a range of topics, from circadian rhythms to Arctic exploration. We drew from primary and secondary sources, including original scientific research in peer-reviewed journals and published works by subject authorities, as well as the popular media. All our sources are carefully cited. Our practice is to identify the source in the body of the text, surround in quotation marks any material taken directly from the source, and provide complete citation information in an endnote.

My team and I also conducted dozens of one-on-one interviews—some with patients of mine who agreed to tell their stories for my book, some with people we found through our personal networks or the media, and some with subject-matter experts. My patients are Brian, Elizabeth, Emma, Gloria, Simon, and Thatcher. The nonpatient interviewees are Alice, Greg, Jenny, Jim, Julia, Lauren, Linda, Marie, Rachel, and Steve. The experts are Betsy Bassett, Shirley Morrissey, Susan Mortweet VanScoyoc, and Jane Rupley. I have been careful to designate my relationship with each individual mentioned in the book.

To protect the identity of the many people who spoke with my team about their experiences, I have changed the names and identifying details about my patients and most of the other interviewees. The only exceptions are Bill and LaDonna Bates, Cass Collins, and Alyson Ewald, whom I call by their real names because they have spoken or written publicly about their experiences, and their work may be a resource for my readers. All of these individuals have given me permission for their stories to be told and their real names to be used.

I should also add that because I maintain my private practices in Boston and Los Angeles, the interviews are skewed somewhat toward New England and California seasons and weather. My team and I have done our best, however, to offset these area-specific stories with research from all over the country and, indeed, all over the world.

The
Emotional
Calendar

Introduction

∽

To be interested in the changing seasons is
a happier state of mind
than to be hopelessly in love with spring.

—GEORGE SANTAYANA, *Reason and Art*

OR MANY YEARS, my wife and two daughters and I spent as much of the summer as we could at our cottage on the beautiful island of Nantucket, off the coast of Massachusetts. I would commute from Boston, where I maintain my practice, sometimes getting away for long weekends to spend more time by the ocean with my family. A psychiatrist's workload is often lighter in the summer months, especially August, when students are away and many patients are able to take some vacation time and try to leave their troubles behind them.

The fact that people are a little less in need of psychiatric help in the summer gives us a clue as to the importance of the time of year to people's emotional well-being. I, for example, usually feel good at the beginning of the summer. When I was on Nantucket, especially, I rarely felt gloomy or out of sorts. I lingered about in the morning, went to the beach for lunch, took a run, and most often prepared a barbeque dinner. Of course, we weren't completely carefree, but sometimes it felt pretty close. I knew I was lucky to be able to enjoy that place and that time with my family and friends.

But the summer holiday was not completely idyllic for me. Year after year, I experienced an irksome period during the last two weeks of August. As Labor Day approached, I would start to feel anxious and ill-tempered. I couldn't enjoy the beach as much as I had earlier in the month. The cooler winds felt biting rather than refreshing. I became distracted and sometimes irritable. Still, we were all together and I was not so intolerable that my behavior was disruptive or that my family made any remarks about it, that I can remember. Nor did I take very serious note of my own mood.

Until, that is, the year my cousin Sally and her family came to visit at the end of August. I love Sally like a sister, and our families get along extremely well. They had visited us on Nantucket in prior years, but always at the beginning of the month. (That particular summer they couldn't get to the island until later.)

Sally's family slipped into the relaxed routine, but I found I couldn't fully join in. Renting bikes at the bike shop, going for ice cream after dinner, discovering new sights on the island—these seemed like foregone pleasures to me. Sally's upbeat determination, which I usually found amusing, irritated me instead. I was annoyed that my children seemed to want to spend their last summer days with their own friends on the beach rather than with their cousins or, for that matter, with me. The cool breezes gave me a bitter emotional chill. I started thinking about September and all the work that lay ahead. I maintain private practices in Boston and Los Angeles, I'm on the faculty at Harvard Medical School and the David Geffen School of Medicine at UCLA, and I have a number of other professional responsibilities that keep me busy. I knew I would not be seeing as much of my family as I would like during the fall. Sally's visit seemed more like an intrusion than a pleasure. I began to feel anxious, fidgety, and crankier than I had in any previous year.

A few days after Sally's arrival, the day dawned gray. Rather than go to the beach, we ate breakfast in town and then looked around the shops. As we wandered from gift shop to clothing store, I felt myself growing more and more on edge. Finally, I made some excuse, hopped on my bike, and headed home. As I rode, I stewed. Why did Sally's visit seem to be ruining my holiday, when normally I enjoyed her company so much? Why did I feel the urge to pack a bag, catch a ferry, and head back to Boston?

As I turned into our driveway, the sun emerged from behind its cloud. I propped my bike against the fence and looked out over the ocean. I took a deep breath. What was going on? Why was I feeling so much stress in such a beautiful place during such a special time of the year? I realized that my crankiness had nothing to do with Sally and her family, or their visit, or my vacation. I was being pulled by conflicting emotions. On the one hand, I wanted to go back to June and July, when my holiday was just beginning. On the other hand, I was already mentally in September, worrying about the work I had to do, and unable to relax. I remembered how I had felt as a teenager, going off to a new school for the first time. I had felt the same anxiety then, wondering how on earth I would get through the next phase of my life, while feeling a sense of regret that a pleasing time was coming to an end. But I wasn't a teenager anymore and I still had most of a good week of vacation left. I shook off my crankiness and determined that I would get myself back together. When everyone returned from town, it had warmed up enough for a swim, so we packed a lunch and spent the rest of the afternoon on the beach. I can't say that my anxiety completely disappeared, but I kept my crankiness in check and found much to enjoy in those last few days of summer.

That moment of realization is as fresh in my mind today as if it happened yesterday. And, although I have since learned how to get through my anxious time at the end of summer much better, that period of the year is still difficult for me, lurking on the calendar, waiting to disrupt the smooth flow of my life. Even though I have identified it and think I understand what it's all about, it can still catch me off guard.

What was happening to me at the end of summer happens to all of us, at different times and in different ways, throughout the year. We all have our own very personal emotional calendars. They differ from the calendar we hang on the wall with its twelve neat pages, each with a photo that reminds us of the traditional idea of the month (September harvest, December holidays, April flowers); they aren't at all the same as our Outlook program, where our appointments and events are so tidily marked. The days and times of year that are most important on our personal emotional calendars don't necessarily line up with the dates and seasons defined on the "official" calendar—the religious observances, national holidays, and natural phases of the sun and moon. These hotspots and misalignments can make us anxious, put us in turmoil, and cause us pain.

Year after year, people get blindsided by dates on their emotional calendars. Most of us muddle through until we start to feel better again. Sometimes, we find ourselves in a more troubling state and have difficulty getting out of it. We're a little dysfunctional for a period of time. We may withdraw. We may be unable to fully engage in some event or activity that is, or could be, meaningful to us. If left unaddressed, these problems tend to become more deeply rooted.

What creates our emotional calendars? That is the subject of this book and, as we'll see, there are a number of factors involved. The seasons and how we feel about them are major influences, especially when our feelings don't quite conform to the traditional ones associated with the season. Another aspect of the seasons, of course, is the environmental characteristics that come along with the weather itself, and we'll see how hot and cold, light and dark, and wind and storms touch our emotions and influence our behavior.

But the most complicated and deeply felt dates on our emotional calendars are the ones that have personal emotional connections. These all, in some way, have to do with our memories—general associations we have with seasons past or recollections of specific events and their connections with the time of year in which they happened.

It is not a problem that we have these emotional calendars—they are the story of our lives, after all. My goal in writing this book is to help people become more aware of their own emotional calendars and those of the people around them. I also hope to show that we can lessen the disruptive influence of those most troublesome times on our calendars and, given some care and mindfulness, learn to live our days and weeks and years with a greater sense of grace and seasonal embrace.

I

⌒

The Emotional Calendar

Spring passes and one remembers one's innocence.
Summer passes and one remembers one's exuberance.
Autumn passes and one remembers one's reverence.
Winter passes and one remembers one's perseverance.

YOKO ONO, "Season of Glass"

T O UNDERSTAND YOUR emotional calendar you probably have to start thinking differently about your life than you do now—not as a steady drumbeat of days, weeks, months, and years, but as a succession of periods of time of varying lengths, each one with a different combination of influences coming into play. Our emotional calendars are far less structured than our daily planners are—sometimes more subtle in their effect and sometimes more dramatic, but often far less predictable. They're harder to manage and can cause us trouble, but they are also rich in emotion and meaning.

We have become accustomed to thinking of the year as a

regular cycle of days and seasons, because we have to do this to keep ourselves organized and functioning and to help us make sense of the world and our lives. So, for example, in the United States and most Western countries, we agree that the year "begins" on January 1. Over the millennia, we have designated a number of religious holidays that punctuate the year—with Christmas a prominent exclamation mark in many societies— and secular ones as well. We live by such social conventions as birthdays and anniversaries. We follow the habit of thinking of the four seasons as if they were well defined, beginning and ending promptly on the appointed calendar date.

These dates and times and milestones tick by each year, giving us structure and a sense of stability. Believe me, I live by my Outlook, my pocket planner, and my BlackBerry. I have patients who expect to find me in my office when they show up for a session. I have two daughters who just may want to spend time with me during their school breaks. I teach a class at Harvard that lasts for fourteen weeks in the fall. We usually try to spend part of the holidays with my wife's family. Our wedding anniversary is an important date. And on and on. So I am as driven as anyone is by the "paper" calendar.

But I also know that the paper calendar doesn't come close to capturing all of the events that I will be living through in the weeks ahead, nor does it have any way to mark the important milestones that will have an effect on me. This is true for most of us, as I have learned from my patients. For example, many people consider the real start of the year to be the first day of school, not January 1, and their lives revolve around that day. We also know that each season varies quite substantially from year to year and, what's more, there can be many seasons within each season. In the Northeast, we may get lucky enough to have a fall that starts in September with crisp air and sparkling light and marches resolutely toward a first December snowfall. The snow may accumulate steadily to a high point in February and then begin to melt away until the first crocus appears. But the seasons rarely proceed in such a predictable fashion. Summer may drift for weeks into September, and we've had heavy snowstorms in May. Each season may feel like a year unto itself.

But these fluctuations and vicissitudes often pale in comparison to the intensity of occasions filled with tremendous personal meaning and rich associations. These can relate to extended periods of your life, such as a time spent living in a certain place or a period marked by an important relationship with a lover, perhaps, or a mentor. They may also be more distinct days or even moments, such as the day you received great news or, as one of the people in this book relates, the minutes spent watching in horror as the World Trade Center was attacked.

There is so much coming at us as we travel along our paths!

How do you come to understand your emotional calendar? How do you recognize the hotspots and difficult times? How do you ameliorate their effects? How do you learn to live with the anxious times with more ease and grace?

In order to make a start on the answers to these questions, let me introduce you to Emma, a wonderfully intelligent and funny young woman, who has been my patient for six years. To meet her, you might not suspect how much she struggles with her emotional calendar. The seasons, especially fall and winter, are particularly tough for her. Her story demonstrates how complex and unique our emotional calendars are; it also shows how the elements of everyone's calendar are very much the same.

Emma: Going Through the Motions

Emma is twenty-one years old and a junior at a prestigious New England liberal arts college where she majors in psychology. She first came to see me when she was fifteen and having a very bad year. She had been attending a prep school outside of Boston, well known for its stringent academics and pressure-cooker environment.

"I think I've had depression since about fourth grade," Emma recalls. "But it got really bad in the middle of my ninth-grade year, and then it just went totally downhill." Emma became seriously depressed and could not continue at the school. She took some time off, did a stint in the hospital, and then transferred to another school that was better able to help with her emotional and psychological issues.

What was going on? It took some time for us to work through the many issues involved, and we're still doing so. To begin with, Emma has always had problems with school. "I can't really remember when I was little very well," she says, "but I've never liked school that much. It's always been very stressful for me. School is always something I just dreaded. I could never really manage it—I was so stressed all the time. Even in preschool, I only went about two days a week. In kindergarten the only reason I made it through was because they bribed me with stickers. I had a very nice collection by the end!"

Emma began to associate her difficulties with school with the change of the season from summer to fall. "It starts around September or late August when I know that it's starting to change into fall," she says. "I notice it's starting to get darker. It's not necessarily a feeling of hopelessness, but more like an absolute dread that I know that this time of year is approaching and I'm not going to feel as happy. My mood is going to go down."

Emma's dread of the school season seems to be magnified by the environmental conditions around her. "I know it sounds kind of weird, but I don't like it when there aren't leaves on the trees," she says. "The angles of the light, the trees are bare, and everything looks so ugly and dead. You can see all the skeletons of the trees. And there's something about it that's just incredibly depressing. It just looks like death. You know, it's horrible."

Emma is exquisitely sensitive to her surroundings and starts to withdraw in the early part of the fall. "Sometimes I wish I could just hibernate through the winter. Actually, that's almost what I do. So on a typical day I'll wake up, I'll get ready for school, I'll go to school, I'll say hi to people. It's like I go through the motions. Maybe it snows and I say, 'Oh hey! I'll have a hot chocolate.' But compared to the summer it's totally different. It's like I'm not really living."

The grimness of the fall is made all the more difficult for Emma to deal with because she loves spring and summer so much. "Spring is a great time of year," she says. "I love it when the green leaves are out and you can see the light filtering through them. I don't like direct sunlight. I find that harsh light to be hard to deal with. But when it's filtered through the leaves, it's very pleasant and that makes me feel good." Summer, too, is a beautiful time for Emma. "During the summer I actually live," she says. "And it feels so good to be alive. You can just exist in summer and you don't even have to do anything necessarily to really enjoy it. The weather invites you to take part in life."

Sensitivity to light, particularly the despondency that sets in during the darker days of fall and winter, is one of the symptoms of seasonal affective disorder (SAD). Emma was diagnosed with the condition some years before we met, and she had already begun using a sunlamp to help alleviate those effects. Indeed, one of the main reasons that Emma first came to see me was that she was convinced that her SAD was at the root of most of her problems, and she was concerned that the sunlamp wasn't enough to keep her depression and morbid thoughts at bay. It took a while for the two of us to unpack all of the deeper issues contributing to her emotional state.

Emma's dislike of winter and love of spring and summer go back a long way. She remembers a favorite book from her childhood called *The Journey Home*.[1] "It's about these two kids," she says. "They go to different places in the world. They go through a hole in their sandbox and visit different mystical creatures. They eat different foods and stay in different beds. I like that book a lot. But, you know, it takes place in the spring. They visit Santa Claus in the winter, but I kind of skip over that part."

So Emma's troubles with fall and winter stem partly from her school problems and partly from her physical responses to the light and look of things, and they have been present since childhood. But there are other issues she contends with as well. She has a particular difficulty with Christmas, not because of the usual holiday issues but because of an emotionally devastating event that took place on that day.

"I was in an abusive relationship with a boyfriend," Emma says. "I didn't really realize it was abusive at the time, but it was. And he broke up with me on Christmas Day. He said that he had been using me for the past three years—that he had never loved me and he was just using me for sex." Emma believes she has gotten over that guy, and she now has a new boyfriend in her life. But the way she talks about the experience suggests that her feelings during winter months are still affected by that painful breakup.

Emma's emotional calendar may sound like a particularly complicated one, and she has certainly had her share of serious emotional difficulties. However, her situation is not uncommon. The fact is that most people—between 70 and 90 percent of us—experience at least one significant trauma during our lifetimes,[2] and there's a good chance that it will have an effect on our emotional calendars. What's more, about 26 percent of people in the United States suffer from a diagnosable mental disorder of some kind.[3] So Emma's emotional calendar is probably more complex than yours or mine, but she is far from alone in her travails. Keep in mind, however, that the emotional calendar is not fundamentally about mental illness or severe depression. Rather, Emma's story illustrates how intensely the seasons and their associations can affect all of us.

These days, Emma is more aware than most of us about the cyclical repercussions of a personal emotional calendar. Most of us focus more on factors that seem to affect us immediately or powerfully while underestimating or ignoring the subtler underlying issues: the events in our past that continue to haunt us years later; the common weather occurrences that don't seem to bother anyone else; the calendar events that we try to enjoy because it seems like we should.

As was the case for Emma, it can take a good deal of introspection and work to recognize the multifaceted and overlapping nature of the dates on your emotional calendar, and even more to understand the way these interact to affect you both physically and emotionally.

So let's pull apart the emotional calendar a little bit. There are two main aspects that compose it: our need for *homeostasis*, or physical stability, and the *emotional hotspots* that are individual to each one of us.

Homeostasis:
The Need for Physical Stability and
the Factors That Disrupt It

Homeostasis is a scientific term that refers to the tendency of a system—usually, a living system—to regulate its internal environment in order to maintain a stable, constant condition. The need for physical stability is the most fundamental of human requirements. The term comes from scientific articles published by Walter Bradford Cannon during the 1920s, and scientists have been refining it ever since. Today, it is understood that factors ranging from temperature and insulin to emotional distress can all impact homeostasis.[4]

The term "dynamic equilibrium" is also often used to describe the body when it achieves balance. I like this phrase because it suggests both balance and constant motion, like the currents beneath an apparently calm lake. Because the world around us is constantly changing as we eat and work and sleep, our bodies are always making dozens of minute changes in our system to keep us in balance.

A good deal of our energy is expended each day just trying to keep ourselves at or near a condition of homeostasis. Maintaining homeostasis is the never-ending task of a regulatory system that is managed by the brain. This remarkable and essential system is not unlike a home thermostat, although a great deal more complicated. When the temperature inside your house gets uncomfortably low, the thermostat communicates the information to your heating system. It is activated and warms the house in response. Once the desired temperature has been reached, the thermostat communicates with the heating system to turn off. In the case of human beings, the thermostat is the brain. More specifically, it is the section of the brain called the hypothalamus, which sits just inside the two tracts of the optic nerve and just above the pituitary gland— that is, behind our eyes.

Achieving and maintaining homeostasis is no easy thing, because it is constantly being disrupted by environmental factors around us. Depending on where we live and our own unique biology, these powerful "physical destabilizers" can threaten our body's homeostasis. They include factors such as sunlight, temperature, and humidity; the presence of pollen and other allergens; barometric pressure; and, some suggest, even the cycle of the moon.

Physical destabilizers impact our health, our comfort, and our sense of balance and well-being. Seasonal affective disorder is one of the most well-known manifestations of the destabilizing influence of the environment, but it is a comparatively rare condition. All of us, however, experience a range of physical and emotional responses to even the most everyday conditions. Shifts in weather and climate affect all of our physical systems, including our pulmonary, gastrointestinal, and reproductive systems, our immune functions, hormone secretion, and more. People exhibit recurring variations in blood pressure, sexual activity, and menstrual cycles depending on the time of year. Births, deaths, suicides—all tend to fall into cyclical or seasonal patterns.

For our purposes, the most important of the destabilizers to homeostasis are light and dark, hot and cold, wind and storms. These are often associated with particular seasons, but they are not completely defined by or contained within any one, and these specific factors can affect us more than the generality of any one season. Although we're all aware of the shifts in the seasons and changes in environmental conditions, most of us are far less cognizant of how those physical shifts affect our emotions and behaviors.

Surprisingly, psychiatrists and scientists have not thoroughly explored the hard links between physical factors and the emotional reactions they cause. As Louis J. Battan, a former professor of atmospheric science at the University of Arizona, writes in his book *Weather in Your Life*, "The psychological effects of the atmosphere are even more difficult to understand than are the physiological ones. The correlation of temperature, pressure, and humidity with certain physical ailments can be examined in controlled laboratory experiments. But the role of the weather in influencing human behavior requires observations of how people respond to preceding or coincident environmental events."[5]

Although this is not a book about weather, per se, weather is certainly an important factor in our emotional calendars. Weather conditions can influence our behaviors, just as the onset of winter affects Emma physically and emotionally.

Emotional Hotspots:
Times of Intensity and Anxiety

Emotional hotspots are those times and events that we accumulate as memories over the years and that become associated with particular physical conditions or with specific periods or seasons on the paper calendar.

These hotspots can be formed in a variety of ways. Some of them are associated with events or periods that take place in the world around you, such as holidays, the school year, or a sports season. Others are much more particular to you and have to do with times of your life, such as a love affair or a time spent living in a different place, or a specific event, such as the death of someone close to you or the day you received your diploma.

Hotspots may be positive or negative; often they are complicated, with both pleasurable and distressing aspects. Above all, when they flare up they are capable of producing intense emotions. Christmas had become a particularly powerful hotspot for Emma, a day when her difficulty with school, hatred of wintry days, and memory of her terrible breakup with her boyfriend all converged.

SEASONALITIES: THE PAPER CALENDAR

Every community has a cycle of shared events and seasonalities that play a role in everyone's emotional calendar. Seasonalities are seasonally related trends that are widespread among a large number of people in the general population. These are usually related to specific and tangible cultural events, including holidays and well-defined time periods, such as the school season. Although you may never have thought about it, your own psychological state is almost certainly linked to seasonal cultural markers, whether you feel a growing dread as Hanukkah approaches or a nostalgia for summers past every Memorial Day and Labor Day. For Emma, the start of the school year is always a difficult time, as is Christmas; while the cause of her trouble is unique to her own experiences, many people have similar anxieties at those times of year.

One of the reasons that whole cultures can get caught up in similar emotions during a particular season is that, as social creatures, we are well adapted to living in groups. Humans take note of and are influenced by the behaviors of others. Social contagion—the tendency to adopt the responses of those around us—is widespread. We tend to feel better when we find ourselves in like-minded company. Even counterculturalists tend to find one another and form their own group subcultures. Participating in seasonal traditions is, therefore, generally comforting.

Seasonalities are not always linked to holidays or specific events; they can also be related to social, cultural, or other kinds of man-made seasons. The various periods of the academic calendar (back to school, exam time, spring break, graduation) are some of the most obvious and significant seasonalities that are not linked completely with one of the natural seasons—although they are certainly associated with and influenced by them. Sports seasons, too, have widespread importance. There are the busy and slow seasons in various professions, the seasonal hobbies that we look forward to, and the seasons we dread, such as tax season and college application time. For some people, these cultural seasonalities are more significant than the traditional seasons themselves.

In addition to those relatively well-known and well-recognized markers, there is also a vast and startlingly diverse number of other kinds of seasonalities: patterns and events that recur at various intervals throughout the year. There is, for example, an alcohol seasonality—more people try alcohol for the first time in December and January than during any other months of the year.[6] There is a sexuality seasonality: more couples have unprotected sex in the summer than at any other time of year.[7] And there are seasonalities that are only obliquely related to actual seasons: travel seasons, fashion seasons, television and movie seasons, and so on.

Different types of crime, too, seem to occur in predictable seasonal patterns. Researchers at Carnegie Mellon University have demonstrated that, in cities, crimes against property (such as burglary and theft) peak during the fall and winter, while crimes of aggression (including assaults, homicides, and rape) rise in the summer and decline in January.[8]

Similarly, the rise and fall of violence in Iraq during the war has been linked to the seasons. Kevin Drum, writing for CBS News, found that violence tended to peak in spring, decline during summer, spike again in autumn, and fall during the winter months. The peaks may have been overemphasized due to the increased violence and casualties in April and November of 2004 but, even without that, the seasonality pattern was quite distinct and traceable. Casualties in July were approximately 40 percent lower than their April peak.[9]

PERSONAL MEMORIES AND MILESTONES

Personal milestones are our own individual associations with specific times of the year. Each of us has a lifetime of memories and experiences upon which our current reality is shaped. The anniversary of a loss or significant life change; birthdays and family events; the resonance of childhood memories at any time of year; and any episode in your life that leaves a lasting impression might all be personal milestones.

When we reconnect to a feeling from the past, we actually relive it, often with undiminished intensity. Any of our senses— sight, hearing, smell, touch, taste—may provoke a recollection, a reconnection that takes us back to a moment when something affected us powerfully. A bit of sensory input from the present, when cross-referenced by the brain's hippocampal formation— our encyclopedia of emotional connections based on past experience—can trigger a powerful reaction in the present, instantly preparing us for a replay of our earlier physiological response and mind-set.

Our memories are closely linked to our emotions. This is why emotionally powerful events, such as the death of a relative, moving to a new location, holidays, and celebrations, tend to form the framework of our childhood memories. Fear is recorded as the emotion most associated with remembered experiences; joy ranks second, anger is third, wonder and curiosity is fourth, sorrow and disappointment is fifth, and pain and shame/guilt are tied for sixth.[10]

Take a moment and look outside. Do any of the seasonal details—the view of icicles melting, perhaps, or the smell of fresh-mowed grass or the sound of crunching leaves—trigger a childhood memory for you? Let yourself follow this feeling in order to see more clearly and in more detail where you were when you felt this way before. Can you see it in your mind's eye? Can you describe the textures of the experience? Try to shake it off and think of another trigger in the season and then follow that one back. The memories abound.

Every season is full of many layers of memories. Some memories are particularly poignant, and these hotspots impact our lives in powerful ways. Emma's most significant personal milestone is the anniversary of the end of her abusive relationship. It's an event that has haunted her ever since, rendering her particularly susceptible to depression at that time every year. The focus of the hotspot is Christmas Day—a day that most of us would like to be full of warmth and familial joy, but which for her brings on a feeling of dread and gloom. It may be worse some years than others, and over time the raw emotional devastation of that Christmas has healed somewhat, but each year Emma must acknowledge that she feels a sudden stab of emotion—an almost physical zing—when the memory returns.

Hotspots also imply a sense of expectation: something significant happened before at a certain time, and so we are programmed to associate that time with the feelings that incident inspired. This is what happens with Emma at the start of the school year: as a child she had a difficult time in school, both academically and socially, and she dreaded going back.

Now, as an adult in college, she continues to expect a rocky start to the year, and this causes her feeling of anxious dread to return. Of course, it's not really that clear to her: it's only on a subconscious level that Emma experiences that sense of expectation, so when the dread comes she doesn't realize that it's just a programmed response. After all, her college life is very different from her earlier education; she has a great deal more freedom and is able to build a structure and a social calendar that suit her emotional needs. She has no immediate reason to expect that the start of school will bring on a new set of problems, so the dread is disconnected from the actual events of her life today.

TRIGGERS: MAKING HOTSPOTS BOIL OVER

A trigger is something that causes feelings from the past to emerge, often rather suddenly and unexpectedly. Triggers can be sensory data, such as smells or sounds; they can also be memories or other stimuli, such as the words in a book. They are external factors that influence our internal processes. While a hotspot is there, waiting, at a certain time of year or a particular event, it may not emerge unless a trigger sets it off, usually causing a sense of anxiety, depression, or pain.

As a sufferer of SAD, Emma can experience an early sunset as a trigger. Even as early as August or September, the first time she notices that the days are growing shorter, she may feel a depressive episode coming on. Pictures of winter, especially of snow, are another trigger. "Looking at winter pictures during the spring is horrible," she says. It gives her a physical jolt, as though she's been suddenly plunged back into the depths of winter. Her favorite childhood book, *The Journey Home*, can still boost her mood in winter, although she always skips the part when the characters visit Santa Claus.

Bringing It All Together: Homeostasis and Subjective Well-Being

Although we have just addressed the physical and emotional aspects of the emotional calendar as if they are separate, they are, of course, closely intertwined and much harder to untangle than it might seem. I like to think of homeostasis as something that balances not only our blood sugar and temperature but also our feelings of happiness and sadness, of anxiety and of peace. Physical and emotional factors together keep us stable.

Homeostasis refers specifically to ordinary changes that affect the body: temperature, food intake, shifts in sunlight. Recently, however, scientists have proposed a more holistic concept to understand physical and mental balance. The concept of "allostasis" refers to "stability through change."[11] When we exercise, for example, we need more glucose—and so our "settings" change. Imagine how we maintain allostasis as we get older, or go through periods of stress!

The concept of "subjective well-being," or SWB, is another way of thinking about this physical and emotional conception of homeostasis. It refers to each person's well-being as a sum of all factors, emotional and physical. A group of Australian scientists studied the emotional range of 649 people for six years and found that everyone has a normal SWB, as we might expect. This means that there is a state of normalcy to which we return and a physical and emotional range within which we feel relatively all right.[12] Maybe we're a little sad, a little sick, or maybe we're really excited, but we're not out of control. Scientists rank the average SWB at 75 on a scale of 1 to 100.[13]

There are many things that can influence our subjective well-being. Emotional upheavals, such as births, deaths, love, and violence, can throw us off. So can physical destabilizers, such as bad weather or excess sunshine. In fact, the emotional and environmental factors affecting us aren't always distinguishable. Scientists have found that stress and anxiety have a big impact on our body's physical homeostasis.[14] And loss of physical stability can trigger an emotional response.

The good news is that there can be a positive consequence of getting thrown out of whack physically and emotionally. Developmental theorists from Jean Piaget to Sigmund Freud have argued that when homeostasis is lost, people have the opportunity to develop.[15] They learn, grow, and change. I certainly learned something about myself in my end-of-summer experience, and Emma is one of the wisest young women I know, largely as the result of her struggles with her lack of stability. So although our tendency is to want to keep ourselves nicely stable at all times, it's useful to understand that times of physical or emotional challenge can lead to personal growth—as long as you have the right perspective and enough support!

Although the research into subjective well-being has been dominated by Western scientific perspectives, analysts in many parts of the world have considered the question of what constitutes well-being. In Taiwan, scientists asked 142 undergraduates to answer the essay question "What is happiness?" Interestingly, they found that "intense, hedonic emotions"— such as joy or elation—were not stressed in the answers. Instead, the students defined happiness more along the lines of "being ordinary" and "feeling comfortable with oneself."[16]

One writer uses the term "harmonious homeostasis" to describe this mental state: "Happiness can be defined as a state of harmony within the individual as well as between the individual and his surroundings. . . . The concept of harmonious homeostasis seems to capture the core implication of happiness being a dynamic process of achieving and maintaining a good fit from within to outward."[17]

Most of us do not expect our days to be filled with great gusts of emotion (good or bad), and would not want them to be; rather, we seek stability and normalcy. That's one of the reasons why, when those intense emotions do occur, we remember them so vividly. They are essentially abnormal states of being and take a special place on our emotional calendars.

The Importance of Awareness

So many different factors contribute to one's emotional calendar, there can really be no *right* way to proceed through the year, and there is no one solution or strategy that can help everyone recognize and overcome their physical destabilizers or deal with their individual emotional hotspots and triggers. To learn to proceed through your emotional calendar with more ease and grace, you just need to start by identifying the factors that affect you the most, and why.

When Emma and I first started working together, for example, she felt there wasn't much she could do about her "winter problem" beyond talking with me, finding a helpful medication, and slogging through until spring arrived. When you're down, it's very difficult to see a way to get up. Six years later, she knows that she will likely be wrestling with the dark seasons for the rest of her life, but she has made a lot of progress in becoming aware of what is happening to her and why.

Last January, for example, Emma came into my office with a scowl on her face.

"It's happening again, all right," she told me.

"What is?" I asked.

"The usual stuff. I don't want to get out of bed again."

"But you got here to see me today," I said.

"Because I had to," she replied.

"Not really. But you knew it was the best thing for you to do."

I offered Emma my support in a form that psychiatrists sometimes refer to with the acronym "PERL." It stands for four important aspects of support: partnership, empathy, respect, and legitimization. Let me take a moment to describe those four elements.

One of the most important things that a psychiatrist can offer a patient is partnership: expressing an active commitment to stick together through difficult times. Essentially, I say to Emma and all my patients, "No matter what, I'll be there for you. We'll stick together on this." Knowing they are not alone in their suffering and that they have an ally can be tremendously helpful in relieving some symptoms for many patients. The second aspect, empathy, involves using words to convey an appreciation of how someone is feeling. It can be very comforting to hear phrases such as "It's so hard. You feel awful." Such comments provide the person with an acknowledgment of their emotions and show that you have an understanding of how it feels. In addition to partnership and empathy, support involves respect. That means praising what a person is doing right— what is helping. As I said to Emma, "But you got here!" The intention is to actively point out and support the things that people can do to help themselves through difficult times. And, finally, legitimization means using a medical model to remind the sufferer that the problem is not his or her "fault." In the case of seasonal depression, it is a medical condition that causes Emma to feel fatigued and dispirited, not a personal weakness, not a character flaw or failing.

So just in that brief initial exchange I had offered Emma a lot of support. She knew I would stick with her, that I felt empathy for her, and respected her efforts in dealing with her problem. I could see her start to relax a little.

"It's just so hard," she said.

"I know."

Most of us react to the troublesome times on our emotional calendar as Emma does. When we come into a difficult time of year, we're not quite ourselves, so we have diminished capacity to figure out what's happening and then do something about it. There's a vicious cycle going on—our mood and behavior are not at their best and, because of that, we aren't quite able to figure out why, which intensifies the emotion still further. Pretty soon we're in a state of funk, totally out of sorts, or taking actions that just don't make sense. These emotional escalations can be troublesome because they negatively affect our work, create conflicts in our relationships, and hamper our ability to get on with our lives.

People can recognize recurring difficulties—they complain about the insomnia they experience in early spring, chronic shoulder pain that flares up in dry hot weather, a melancholy that they can't avoid as the New Year approaches—and yet so often they dismiss, ignore, or completely repress the connections between their personal calendar and these experiences.

Why do we permit ourselves to live, year after year, with disruptive patterns engraved in our emotional calendars? As individuals, we respond to emotional disruptions in the same way, over and over again. We allow ourselves to repeat these patterns because familiar habits, even negative ones, help us feel more in control, and any semblance of control is comforting.

In order to break out of these patterns, we need to exchange this illusory sense of control for what I call "adaptive control." The term comes from physics, where it refers to the numerous methods that allow a system to adapt to changes over time.

Adaptive control is what allows an airplane to adjust for loss of mass caused by burning fuel without flying out of control. In psychology, it is the ability to make necessary changes to resolve problems in our lives while maintaining the sense of security we get from being in control. Adaptive control is the ability to *recognize patterns*, to *gain perspective*, and to make *positive choices* that allow us to feel more happy, balanced, and hopeful in our daily lives. I'll talk more about adaptive control and how it works in chapter 12.

Our Relationship with the Seasons Has Changed

A thousand years ago, our lives were inextricably intertwined with the seasons and weather, much more so than they are today. Every aspect of life was governed by the physical realities of the time of year. People virtually hibernated during the dark winter months, when food and light were scarce and snow and ice prevented most travel. During the summer heat, people anticipated that they would be operating at half speed. Even a hundred years ago, we accepted that many foods simply weren't available during three out of four seasons, and everybody knew what ailments or difficulties they were likely to suffer in any kind of weather. The spring rains, they knew, would inflame the joints of those with rheumatism; if the leaves had not fallen by St. Martin's Day (November 11), everyone hunkered down for a cold, harsh winter.[18]

Over the centuries, we have done our best to mitigate and control the effects of the seasons, their associated environmental conditions, and the threats they make to our physical homeostasis and emotional well-being. In the developed world today, however, our relationship with the seasons and seasonalities is different. At any time of the year, we can travel to any kind of weather we choose. We spend most of our days in temperature-controlled environments, and generally move from one to another—from the house to the car or train to the office and back again—with as little exposure to the elements as possible. We still pay a lot of attention to the weather reports, but we care about them mostly as they tell us how to prepare for those few moments of exposure, or how they will affect our vacation or recreational plans.

The seasons, and the weather patterns typical of each, have become almost inconsequential in our daily lives. Yes, a heavy snowfall might inconvenience us, and a forecast of a week of sunny weather might make us more excited for an upcoming vacation but, really, these are trivialities that have only a minimal effect on our daily routines. No matter the time of year, no matter the weather, most of us still go to work at the same time every day; we go food shopping, spend time with loved ones, go to our church or book club or gym. Even the holidays and events that are most important to us are worked into our schedules with as little interruption as possible. For most of us, life is quite consistent throughout the year, and the seasons are simply background—inexorable and endlessly fascinating but, in the end, almost irrelevant.

And yet.

There are certain phenomena that we, both individually and collectively, cannot ignore. After a few days of continuous rain, people begin to stare dolefully out the windows and sigh. When the sun finally comes out again, there is a general sense of relief and good cheer. When a serious hurricane or earthquake hits one city, the whole nation—and sometimes the whole world—tunes in to the news and closely follows reports of damage and losses. On a given day, most people will have at least one conversation about the weather, the season, or the time of year in general. These are behaviors and experiences that we all have in common and are part of a shared experience.

The ability to be aware of our own responses to the seasons largely depends on how in tune we are with the seasons themselves. This can be surprisingly difficult to gauge. We know what each season is *supposed* to be like—and, in fact, we might have very rigid ideas of what the weather should be, how we should feel, and how we should all behave in a given season. But so often the reality simply does not match up to our expectations, both in terms of the weather and in how we feel, and this discrepancy can throw us off far more than we realize.

When people live in the temperature-controlled, artificial environments that so many of us do, it becomes even more difficult to be aware of how we feel about a given season or type of weather, or why. We may realize that the onset of fall makes us anxious and uncomfortable but have no idea whether those feelings stem from some barely remembered past pain, or from physical destabilizers such as decreasing sunlight or the hormonal shifts within our bodies brought on by the changing season. On the other hand, people who live more deeply within the seasons—farmers, for example—might be too literal in their expectations of autumn, based entirely on the weather and the success of the harvest. They might not realize how deep their emotional connection to the season really is.

Moreover, the world around us is changing, and so is our place in it. Climate change is an increasing concern, and with every passing year our lives and livelihoods are being affected by it. The almost limitless access to the world we are given by cell phones, the Internet, Skype, and other technologies has changed the way that many people work and interact with friends and colleagues. For some people, there is no need to ever leave the house if they don't wish to. At the same time, travel is faster and more convenient now than it has ever been, and a great number of people the world over take advantage of this fact, both for work and for pleasure, throughout the year.

I have come to the conclusion that few of us have the relationship with the calendar that we think we do. Even when we feel that we have a handle on things, the world shifts a little bit and our experience changes. In order to achieve a real awareness of your emotional calendar, therefore, it's important to understand that—in addition to all the influences discussed in this chapter—the world has changed and is continually changing; more important, you must develop an honest and accurate perspective of how you personally are influenced by these changes.

Everyone's emotional calendar is incredibly dynamic—constantly changing as the result of physical conditions, cultural seasonalities, shifts in the state of the world, and, of course, new experiences and events that take place in our day-to-day lives. The place to start, though, in coming to terms with your emotional calendar, is in your past. To find out what you are affected by, consider what you've been through.

PART I

The Four Seasons
(You Thought You Knew)

When she came back, the sun was just past its peak, and

it was a bad time of day for her; it'd be better when it got

dark. How she had loved the long evenings of spring

when she was young, and all of life stretched before her.

—ELIZABETH STROUT, *Olive Kitteridge*

 Seasons change: we all know that. The only place where there were truly no seasons (whether hot or cold; wet or dry) was perhaps the Garden of Eden. And it's been a long time since we were living there.

We change, too, in relation to the seasons, not only over the course of a single year but—as the passage above suggests—over the course of our lives.

In places like New England, where I live most of the year, we think of the seasons as four "quarters" of roughly equal length making up the year. This is an easy model we can all wrap our heads around, like the four quarters of the business year. I'm certainly not going to ask you to throw out this useful way of understanding the flow of time, nor do I ever suggest to my patients that they should. How could any of us, unless we were actually dwelling in the Garden of Eden? In fact, keeping track of the paper calendar, and what it holds in store for us, helps us become more aware of our individual emotional calendars.

The issue for many of us is that the seasons carry with them a great deal of cultural baggage. Fall, for example, is about going back to school or work, or some kind of "official" existence, and making something productive of your life. Summer is supposed to be the time of carefree days and steamy nights, youthful pursuits, and romantic adventure. The stereotypes differ from place to place and culture to culture, but there they are.

We have problems with these conventional views of the seasons when we feel out of sync with what society around us is doing, or *seems* to be doing anyway, at a given time. So understanding your emotional calendar is also about unpacking some of that baggage and seeing which parts you really *do* want to keep. In the following chapters we'll focus on the traditional seasons and their emotional and cultural implications. In part 2, I'll write with more depth about the physical and environmental factors that can influence our health, moods, and behavior throughout the year.

The Cycle of the Seasons

We may have departed from the Garden of Eden, but we will not likely escape from the cycle of the seasons. They come about from the earth's yearly movement around the sun. Because the earth's axis tilts at 23.5 degrees off vertical, one area of our planet is always more exposed to the rays of the sun than the others. In the temperate and subpolar regions (including the United States, of course), we get the four classic seasons: summer, fall, winter, and spring. In the tropical and subtropical regions, it is more useful to speak of rainy and dry seasons, because the amount of seasonal precipitation varies more than the temperature. Seasonal changes everywhere are also subject to the effects of large bodies of water, ocean currents, and prevailing winds.

The seasons not only look different from place to place around the world but are spoken of differently as well. In some traditional cultures, the seasons will often be described by observable events such as the flowering of particular plants, when trees bear fruit, and how animals behave. For example, the indigenous Brambuk people in Australia operate with six different periods of the year: early summer, late summer, autumn, winter, pre-spring, and spring. Early summer (mid-November to the end of January in Australia), is defined as the time when "butterflies chase in the warm sun." Late summer (from the end of January to late March) is when the Brambuk observe "snakes basking in the sun" and that "the night is bright with stars."[1]

Harvest times have long been the most fundamental of seasonal markers, and, over the centuries, people developed intriguing habits and practices to celebrate them. In pagan Europe, for example, the first sheaves of grain gathered at the summer solstice (around June 21) and the last sheaves harvested at the fall equinox (around September 22) were braided together and made into dolls called the Corn Mother or Harvest Mother. Some peoples would leave the dolls in the field, hoping they would ensure a good yield the following year; some paraded the dolls through the village for all to see; others burned them on large ceremonial pyres. We all have our individual ways!

All over the world, cultures as diverse as the ancient Celts, imperial Romans, the Aztecs, the Iroquois, and the Nganasans of Siberia celebrated the winter solstice (around December 21) with rituals in which they would extinguish and then relight candles or fires, to symbolize the much-welcomed return of the summer sun. During modern winter holidays, we still carry on many celebrations and rituals that feature candles and fires and lights of all kinds.

Today's developed countries are, of course, industrialized and far less rural and agriculturally centered than they once were. I don't know much about gardening, but I do know that many people are drawn to it because it brings them a connection with the harvest, in particular, and nature, in general, that they find meaningful. Indeed, many people find that gardening is a good way to become more aware of our seasonal moods and of our ancient associations with the natural environment. You'll see many examples of this in the coming chapters.

This brings us to the present "inconvenient truth," as Al Gore calls it, that our natural environment—including the seasons themselves—is changing right before us. Today, as I write this book, the international scientific community has generally accepted that climate change is a reality. If you read the 2007 report by the Intergovernmental Panel on Climate Change (as one of my researchers did!) you will discover that it is likely that, over the past three hundred years, human impact on the environment has resulted in rising sea levels, changes in wind and temperature patterns, dramatic temperature extremes, and increased drought, heat waves, and storms. The report predicts that these changes will continue over the next hundred years. There is the real risk that seasonal shifts of even a couple of weeks will result in "eater" and "eaten" becoming out of sync with each other, spelling disaster for the food chain. Catastrophic weather events such as Hurricane Katrina in New Orleans could well become more frequent around the world.[2]

We all feel the effects of climate change in one way or another, some large and some small, some globally significant and some more personally relevant. One effect that many people have already experienced is climate change's impact on outdoor activities, including the length and quality of recreation seasons. In 2002, for example, Colorado experienced atypical drought and wildfire conditions that caused a sharp decrease in visits to its park systems and a decline in fishing and rafting trips. There were lower than normal water levels on the Great Lakes between 1999 and 2001, which caused a drop in boating. And because of a lack of snow in the Midwest, business at many ski areas was affected.[3] Recreational activities that we may have looked forward to all year are, in some cases, no longer available as much or in the same way as they once were. This shift in our leisure activities can have ill effects on our mental health, especially when so many of us depend on these activities to bring us relief from the day-to-day grind.

But take heart, sports fans, because many other physical activities have gone in the opposite direction—in many popular sports we're experiencing a phenomenon called "season creep." In the United States, for example, the Super Bowl has been pushed forward, from January 9 in 1977 to January 28 in 1996 to February 7 in 2010. In college football, the season has exploded as the number of bowls grew from twenty-two (in 1999) to thirty-four (in 2009).[4] Baseball (a sport I do know something about, being a loyal Red Sox fan and newly initiated rooter for the Los Angeles Dodgers) begins in early April and runs until the World Series, which ended on November 4 in 2009. In 1990, the series ended on October 20. Add to this a never-ending expansion of postseason, preseason, and all-star games, and it's easy to see why *Washington Post* columnist Tracee Hamilton writes, "Even rabid fans are feeling overwhelmed by what I call 'season creep.' Seasons are starting earlier, running later, overlapping more often and generally sucking more of our time than ever."[5]

David Carter, executive director of the University of Southern California's Sports Business Institute, agrees that what used to be defined as "the season" has changed or disappeared entirely in almost every sport. The driving force behind season creep is largely financial: the NFL, for example, generates $8 billion in revenue each year, up from $1.3 billion in 1990. The money would not be there, of course, were there not demand for more sports more of the time. However, concerned officials and players wonder whether season creep will lead to player and fan burnout.[6]

We also used to mark our calendars with the idea of the television season. We'd get thirteen weekly episodes of our favorite sitcom or cop drama starting in the fall and then, if all went well, there would be another batch coming our way in the spring. But the television season, too, is an almost obsolete phenomenon. An article in the *New York Times* pointed out that while the prime-time television season starts in September (this because it was originally linked to car companies introducing new models in this month), the notion of a season has evolved into "lasting all year."[7] At the same time, many shows have very limited or unpredictable runs. The first "season" of the HBO show *In Treatment*, for example, had forty-three episodes, which ran mostly on consecutive nights over a nine-week period starting on January 28, 2008. (Since it featured a psychiatrist as its hero, I was, naturally, quite a fan of the show.) Some people watched the episodes faithfully, and that period of January to March became a kind of miniseason for them. In its second season, *In Treatment* started airing in April 2009. Go figure. It has come to the point that only the Nielsen Company (the company that keeps track of how many viewers are watching which shows) seems to care about when the season starts. The idea of the TV season is further obliterated by the availability of shows in so many other channels and formats—on demand, on DVD, online, on the iPod. People can now discover a show they like and watch an entire season over a weekend or a few days. For them, that period is defined by the show and they can feel a little disconnected from their friends and families who are glued to the screen watching *30 Rock* while they're totally entranced by *Mad Men*.

So all the seasons that surround us—natural, artificial, and in between—are highly dynamic and in a constant state of flux, adding more complexity to both our paper and emotional calendars.

We can begin to explore and unpack our complex seasons— and start seeing them as something more than rigid quarters of the year—by hearing stories from people who experience summer, fall, winter, and spring in very individual and sometimes unexpected ways.

2

Supercharged Summer

> On nights like this we used to swim in the quarry,
>
> the boys making up games requiring them
>
> to tear off the girls' clothes
>
> and the girls cooperating, because they had
>
> new bodies since last summer
>
> and they wanted to exhibit them, the brave ones
>
> leaping off the high rocks—bodies crowding the water.
>
> —LOUISE GLUCK, "Midsummer"

SUMMER IS A supercharged time. For many of us, it carries a tremendous amount of emotional resonance, often tangled up with childhood memories. It is a time filled with expectations of how we should be feeling and behaving, replete with myths and cultural images of carefree times, sunny romance, and childlike happiness. We have a strong sense that summer should be a stretch of unmitigated joy and freedom, even if it has never actually delivered on that promise. At the very least, summer means a change in schedule and, if we're lucky, vacation time. Many relax, try something new, or try to recapture the good old days.

We often set goals for what we'd like to do or achieve or

experience over the summer. They tend to be personal ones and are sometimes overambitious or downright unrealistic.

> "This is the summer I'll meet the right guy (or girl) and fall in love."
>
> "This summer, I'll work out every day and get superfit so when I get back to work no one will even recognize me."
>
> "This summer, I'm going to have the most amazing travel adventure ever."
>
> "This summer, I am going to eat nothing but seasonally grown, organic vegetables and drink nothing but green tea and Fair Trade, shade-grown, organic coffee."
>
> "This summer, I am going to do absolutely nothing I don't want to do and not torture myself about anything."

We can put so much seasonal pressure on ourselves. To develop and safeguard a sense of well-being, it's important to be aware of these unreasonable expectations and find ways to rethink what the season really means to us and what we can realistically expect from it.

Summer Unfolds in Phases

It's interesting to note that summer is an unstructured season, relatively free of official dates and cultural or religious holidays. In the United States, at least, we mark the beginning of the season with Memorial Day (even though summer's official start date isn't for nearly another month) and its end with Labor Day (again, even with the end date still weeks away), but the time in between is remarkably free of special days, other than Independence Day. This pattern generally holds true around the world. If I use my "Add Holidays" feature in Outlook, I see Bastille Day in France (July 14), Independence Day in India (August 15), and Late Summer Holiday in the United Kingdom (August 30). There is a scattering of summer holidays around the globe. But we Americans certainly like to keep our summers free, open, and clear of official obligations as much as possible.

Summer may be unstructured, in terms of official events, but it has relatively distinct phases—early, deep, and waning—as all the seasons do. (In this, we are not unlike those Brambuk people of Australia who identify six different phases of the season.)

In the early phase, as we make plans and finish up the "work" of the spring, life can be pretty hectic. There's a continuation of spring's energy with (we hope) better weather, more natural abundance, and the acknowledgment of summertime. Jane Rupley is a garden designer, and she notices that her profession heats up in May. "People get out there and see their yards again and they're all gung ho for about six weeks," she says. One of her clients called her around Memorial Day and wanted an entire garden designed and installed by the Fourth of July. "It's like a tax accountant—asking them on April fifth or tenth or something to get the whole thing done," Rupley says.[1] Then, around the middle of June, many people lose interest in doing anything new in their garden and calm down again.

In the deep phase of summer, from the Fourth of July onward, my office is at its quietest. Many of my patients have made their seasonal plans, modified their usual routines, and are feeling pretty content with where they are and how they're feeling—or at least they are trying. However, a more fundamental problem with summer usually occurs around this time: we try to reconcile the current summer with summers past. There is always a sense of comparison. Is this summer as wonderful as the one we had three years ago, when we traveled with friends to California? Are my kids enjoying themselves as much as I did when I was twelve? Will they have the same memories I do?

For many, there is room for a quiet resentment that the summers of our adult life are not the summers of our youth. I remember feeling that I was missing out on the pleasures of summertime when I was a house officer and in-patient attending physician early in my career. One day, a cabdriver asked me about my plans for the summer and if I would be doing anything different or special.

"Not really," I answered.

"Well then," he replied, "I guess your summertime isn't going to feel too summery."

Wisdom indeed! Later on, when I had the ability to modify my office hours, I was able to take more time off to enjoy the outdoors in the summer again.

Then comes the waning phase of summer, which, as I know very well, brings its own set of challenges: a sense that, however well the summer has gone, it was not good enough, fun enough, memorable enough. Somehow, it didn't quite match our expectations. Maybe we got fitter but not superfit. We developed a couple of interesting relationships but did not meet the One. We traveled to some intriguing spots but didn't have the amazing experience we hoped for. "Doing nothing" took a lot more work and planning than we thought. And so, as summer starts to slip away, so do our hopes for personal improvement and transcendence. Dreams of leaping off the high rocks settle down.

We struggle to make the adjustment to the next season, the

time of bracing work and crisp focus for many but, as we'll see in the next chapter, a period of near-mania for a few.

Jenny: The Summer Grouch

Not everybody feels sanguine about summer. Some people, like Jenny, can barely stand the sight of it.

Jenny, a forty-eight-year-old mother of two, has a tough time in the summer. She likes working in the garden. She loves having more time with the kids. But when it gets hot, watch out. Jenny feels listless, grows irritable, and has trouble enjoying or even completing daily activities. She has no interest in beaches or bathing suits, pools or other bodies of water. When it gets intolerably hot, she retreats inside, curls up on the couch to read a book, and stays well away from the heat and glaring sun. Jenny jokes that she is the exact opposite of most people, who would prefer to hibernate in the winter and spend the summer outside.

Jenny's trouble with summer is triggered by the first indicator of the heat to come. "You know when you're in college and there's that first day that's even remotely warm and everyone's wearing shorts?" Jenny asks. "That would be the day that I'd think, 'Oh, God, it's coming.'" I can certainly relate to that. That first summery day, especially in college, is an iconic memory for many of us.

A couple of physical factors are at play here. If Jenny spends too much time in bright sunlight she is susceptible to migraines, and she is very sensitive to the extra noise that seems to come with hot weather, when more people are outside and the neighborhood kids are home from school.

"I like to have a lot of quiet in my life," Jenny says. "But in hot weather, you can't get away from the noise. In the afternoons there's a bunch of kids that play on the street, and you hear people's music, and other people out on their decks. I like to have my windows open, I like the fresh air. But I like to be able to control the amount of noise in my life, and it's just harder to do that in the summer."

The hot weather makes her sweaty and uncomfortable, which saps her energy.

"I have this malaise that comes over me when it's really hot and humid, or when I've been in the hot, strong sun a lot. It's both physical and mental. Physically I feel really draggy, like I'm walking through Jell-O. Mentally, I just go into a sort of coping mechanism. I say, 'OK, I just have to make it through this heat wave. Just get to the end of the day and it will be better tomorrow.'"

Jenny is a lawyer. She scaled back her practice when the kids were younger and is now slowly rebuilding her client relationships and taking on more work. While the stress of her career means she has a pretty short fuse all year long, she admits that her grouchiness reaches its peak in the summer. "In the summer I'm just grumpier. It's like PMS—I'm just kind of pissed off."

Although Jenny is quite aware of her summer malaise, she is not particularly skilled at suppressing it, but she finds ways to manage it. Her family is also aware of the difference in her behavior during the summer and her husband, who was raised in Costa Rica and thrives in the heat, is saddened that they will never move to his native country. "I am never going to live there," she says. "He knows that. Never in a million years."

Over the years, Jenny has come to accept that she will spend more time indoors during the summer than other people, and she has learned to withstand the social pressure to get outside and enjoy the sunshine. "I just don't feel like I have to be spending tons of time outside if that's not what I want to do," she says.

To cope better, Jenny pays a lot of attention to the basics of cooling down. The family installed air conditioners in the rooms where she spends most of her time. When she does go outside for an activity of some kind, such as a field day at her children's elementary school, she lugs along a big jug of ice water. "It really makes a huge difference to me."

Drinking ice water in the summer heat may seem like a simple, even obvious, solution to the problem. But it demonstrates the kind of self-awareness that is essential in mitigating our responses to our emotional hotspots. I doubt that Jenny will be moving to Costa Rica any time soon, but I have to applaud her for realizing that the world thinks about summer in one way and she thinks about it in another. And never the twain shall meet.

A Different Kind of SAD in the Summer

Summer can cause trouble for people in other ways as well. Most people have heard about seasonal affective disorder, or SAD, the problem that Emma was dealing with, and I'll talk a little more about the issues associated with sunlight deprivation in chapter 7.

The "regular" SAD is always associated with winter, but there is also a summer version, called "reverse" or "tropical" SAD. This is the misery some people feel in the extremely hot, humid weather common to tropical parts of the world. Dr. Shirley Morrissey, a clinical and health psychologist at Griffith University's School of Applied Psychology in Queensland, Australia, has done fundamental research in this area, which, interestingly, came out of an observation that pertained more to the cultural aspects of the season than to the physical ones. She saw that "everyone is supposed to look forward to summer"—even though some people clearly do not.

Morrissey gathered data from some two hundred adults in Townsville, the largest city in northern Australia, where summer lasts from November through March and is characterized by high heat, lots of humidity, and rainfall similar to that of a monsoon. She found that just over half the sample (53.9 percent) reported that they felt at their worst during one or more months of summer. Nine percent reported that the impairment they felt was bad enough to warrant a diagnosis of tropical SAD.[2] What's fascinating is that this percentage correlates to the occurrence of winter SAD in temperate climates.

However, Morrissey believes that unlike winter SAD, which is generally thought to be caused by light deprivation and for which phototherapy can help, changes in sunlight exposure are probably not the primary cause of tropical SAD. "Studies have been done to try and correlate what it is in our climate that causes SAD—too much light, or heat, or humidity," she explains.[3] "But no correlations have been established. My own opinion is that it's the combination of heat and humidity. Some people are just very sensitive to this, more sensitive than others." Her research has also established that there is also no connection between tropical SAD and overall neurosis, though many people assume there is. "I think it's biological, and not a question of personality," she concludes.

In a related study, Morrissey asked forty-three people to keep diaries of how the weather affected them during the winter and summer seasons, for ten weeks total.[4] Of these, twenty-three participants were "seasonal," in that they reported they were affected by the weather. Seventeen were "nonseasonal," reporting they were not affected by the weather. All the participants took notes about how much they slept, ate, drank, and so on—the main bodily functions—as well as how they generally felt in relation to the weather each day. A few representative comments:

> "I feel irritable. Writing in this diary is making me realize how my irritability is connected to the weather."
> "I hate sitting in traffic when it's this hot."
> "I don't feel like doing anything. Everything seems too difficult to do in the heat."

But then rain arrives, bringing reprieve from the malaise of tropical summer. You can practically feel the new air (and renewed energy) coming up from the page.

> "The rain came finally, cooling everything down. Finally, I felt like I could do things again."

A Riskier Attitude Toward Sex

Summer can entice people to do things they might be less inclined to do otherwise. Our sense of summer as a time of freedom and abandonment affects many of our most fundamental behaviors, including our sex drive. The likelihood of premarital first sex, for example, among teens and especially among teenage girls, has been shown to be highest in summer, at least according to some studies. (And, of course, it makes some intuitive sense.) One study in Brazil showed that between 1992 and 1997, more unmarried girls—36 percent—became sexually active in the summer than in any other season.[5]

A study commissioned by the Department for Education and Skills in Great Britain says that two factors contributed to the rise in sexual activity during the summer: first, easy access to alcohol and, second, the "suspension of reality" brought on by the heady sense of freedom of summer at the beach. One result is that seaside resort towns have some of the highest teenage pregnancy rates in Britain: Blackpool had 75 conceptions per 1,000 girls aged fifteen to seventeen, in comparison to the national average of 43. Other resort towns such as Torbay, Southend-on-Sea, Brighton, and Hove had rates of conception from 10 to 44 percent higher than the national average.[6]

The Power of Summers Past

The emotional power that summer holds over us can be most clearly seen, perhaps, in older people who remember the way they experienced the season in a different time.

Greg, for example, lives alone in a house he built for his family back in 1951. At eighty-nine, he remembers ice-skating on the nearby river, when it used to freeze solid, trips to the West Coast, and other family activities. But most of all, he thinks about his summers on Nantucket. Back in the day, Greg's wife would travel with the kids to Nantucket just a few days after school let out and spend the whole summer season there, and Greg would join them on weekends as he could. (Sounds familiar!) The whole family enjoyed activities such as swimming and boating. But I was struck by a specific memory he had of sitting with his wife on the upstairs deck of their still-unfinished home—or "shack," as he describes it—looking out at the ocean as the fog rolled in. "The only sound was the foghorn going," he recalls. "And we decided, well, that's what it's all about." Something about this deep sense of contentment coalesced in that summer moment looking out to the water, and he has held on to the memory for decades. But now, he comments regretfully about how ritzy and built-up Nantucket has become, a place full of "castles." He hasn't gone there much since his wife went to assisted living and then to a nursing home.

This traditional family story strikes me powerfully, largely because it harkens to an experience of summer that is fast fading away. Summer vacations have changed dramatically over the past couple of decades. People tend to take shorter vacations and, when they do go away, they often take work with them. A study by American Express showed that many small business owners, for example, try to combine business and pleasure travel, primarily to save time and money. Among business owners planning a summer break, about 33 percent will link vacations with business trips.[7]

Rarely do families go away to summer homes or camps or other retreats for the whole summer as they used to. We don't have the time anymore. In the majority of families, both spouses work, so coordinating schedules for even a couple of weeks together can be challenging. There are so many more options than there used to be—travel has gotten cheaper and become more available, and there is an endless variety of activities that people want to pursue. The do-nothing vacation of lying for hours on the beach under the sun is also out of favor, partially due to health concerns about overexposure to ultraviolet rays, partly because people want to fill their time with more action.

Whether we love summer or hate it, look forward to it or backward upon it, summer remains an emotionally charged time, filled with hope and disappointment, a likely hotspot on many emotional calendars. Just the fact that summer was the out-of-school time we used to look forward to so much and that so few of us now get to enjoy as fully as we would like (with the possible exception of some teachers and those fortunate to work on an academic schedule), explains a lot about the significance of summer. So ask yourself what your summers were like. What do you carry with you from summers past? What do you want—realistically—for next summer? By exploring these questions and coming to some realizations, you'll be better able to consider what you can do to effect positive changes for the future.

3

The Reality of Fall

There is a great difference between this season and a
month ago—warm as this happens to be—as between
one period of your life and another. A little frost is at
the bottom of it.

—HENRY DAVID THOREAU, *Journal*, October 7, 1851

"A LITTLE FROST is at the bottom of it"—I love that line. It expresses both the emotional and physical sense of this tricky season.

While fall can be a time of great energy and change, it is also a bracing dose of sobriety for most of us. From the sense of unstructured summertime, whether we enjoy it or can't wait for it to end, autumn is a return to reality: back to work, back to school, back to the routine, whatever it might be. While we may be energized by the seasonal change, we may also feel that it is a period that requires preparation, encourages taking stock, and provokes us to want to improve our situation.

The significance of going back to school came up again and

again in our conversations with my patients and with others. Why wouldn't it? Starting at the age of five, and for many of us even before that, we have trundled off to school every September. For the majority of Americans—about 85 percent—this schedule continues through the end of high school. Any pattern that plays out over a period of twelve to fifteen years, especially early in life, is bound to leave an imprint. And a good percentage (about 29 percent) of Americans continue on to get a bachelor's degree,[1] while a smaller amount keep at it until they have earned an advanced degree. For me, the "school years" continued into my early thirties. I figure I made it through the twenty-fifth grade, with four years of college, another four in medical school, and an additional five years completing my residency training and fellowship.

The summer-fall transition was, and still is, a difficult one for me, and it was for Emma, too. She vividly remembers the stickers that were used to "bribe" her to leave the house and board the bus to kindergarten. In the next chapter, we'll meet Brian, who also had a tough time going back to school. For him, it meant the end of barefoot days and the beginning of an ongoing battle with the nuns at his school, who gave him a hard time about his stuttering. Memories of this annual rite of return in early September don't go away easily, if at all. Many people continue to see their year as "beginning" in fall. The Jewish calendar does, in fact, begin in fall, reinforcing this pattern for some. And even if you are long past school days, your children will start the familiar cycle in your family all over again.

Most people feel a surge of energy, a need for increased productivity and new challenges come fall. It's not just the back-to-school ethos; it's the weather, too: in most areas of the country, the days are crisp, or at least crisper. Conditions beget a clear head, a vision of purposefulness and accomplishment. The body feels in balance; fall seems to be a time of homeostasis.

We like to think of autumn as a time for the establishment of order. But as energizing as autumn can be, it can also seem overwhelming—too much to do, too many expectations, too little time before we find ourselves back in the throes of winter. As a result, people often feel a sense of conflict, not just with the summer that has fled all too quickly, but with the winter that is approaching too fast. This can lead to a kind of overexcitement and an inability to actually enjoy the season as it unfolds.

Fall is additionally complicated by the many holidays and celebrations that take place in these months. In contrast to summer, with its almost complete lack of holidays, fall is full of them all around the world: Labor Day; Rosh Hashanah, Yom Kippur, and Sukkot; Chuseok (the Korean harvest festival); Diwali (the Hindu festival of lights); Thanksgiving Day in the United States. It can be a destabilizing brew.

Marie: The Big Shutdown

My friend Marie always surprises me. She is a busy woman in her forties, a partner in a real estate development and management company who spends most of her time in one office or another. But she is amazingly in tune with the natural world.

At the end of an unseasonably cool summer in New England, the heat had returned for a few days, but Marie could feel the onset of fall. "You can feel it right now," she says. "It's getting dark between seven thirty and eight o'clock. A month ago it was getting dark at nine." For Marie, summer peaks at the solstice—June 21—when the hours of daylight are at their longest. By July 4, when everybody else thinks that summer is really getting going, Marie is starting to feel that the season is winding down, and fall seems uncomfortably inevitable.

Not that the early phase of fall is all that bad for her. In fact, Marie has incredible memories of back-to-school shopping with her mother. "That was such a big thing. It was so exciting," she says, smiling at the memory. "New sweaters and pants. The whole shopping experience with my mom was a big thing in our family." Fall shopping meant more than clothes. It also meant that special excitement of new school supplies: notebooks, pens, the pencil case, and erasers.

Marie can still feel the excitement and pressure of schoolwork again as if it's happening in real time. "It's a childhood memory that's totally alive," she says. "Sunday nights and the panic of Monday. Had I really gotten all my homework done, and ooh, God, I hadn't. How was I going to allocate the time? Was it going to be French or math or chemistry?"

But mostly the fall air holds sadness for Marie. In summer, she enjoys farm stands filled with local produce. "And then, all of a sudden, you drive by and see this place filled with pumpkins or Christmas trees. And then they shut down. That's it. There's just a gray wood bench with nothing on it. Everything shuts down."

Marie always feels the urge to get away around October, to escape what she knows is coming. "Everybody's done their back-to-school thing. Now I've got to go somewhere, too. I have to ward off the darkness in the winter and the seasons and, I don't know, the whole holidays. I like the holidays, but that Thanksgiving-to-Christmas month is such a panic."

The Crisp Fresh Air:
Autumn Seasonalities

For many, autumn overlaps with one of the most powerful cultural seasonalities: football. The sport begins in September and runs through January or February, overlapping with the baseball play-offs and the World Series in October. Fall's cool, sunny weather can be ideal for outdoor sports, and high school, college, and professional football have made the sport a favorite autumn activity.

Fall is also the hunting season. While turkeys are hunted in spring, most animals, including deer, waterfowl, moose, and bears, are hunted in the fall.[2] Hunters and athletes alike tend to associate the physical aspects of fall—fresh cool breezes, changing leaves, even ice-cold rains—with nostalgia for a youth spent outdoors.

Rod Davis, in an article for *Virginia Hunting Today*, remembered his first hunting trip with his father: "It was one of those early autumn, blue bird perfect days that cause your nose to breathe a little harder than usual, just to get more of that crisp, clean air inside. It was the kind of day that you would look forward to all summer, and remember for many seasons to come."[3] For Davis, the memory is profound. He describes his first shot, a gray squirrel.

> I walked downhill to see where the little fellow went and lo and behold, there he was a still grey lump lying in the leaves. I reached to pick him up and he twitched and tried to crawl away. I watched in horror as the little squirrel died.
>
> My days as a hunter nearly ended right then and

there. It was there on that hillside that two deep changes occurred inside a young boy. First a lifelong love affair with hunting was born, and second, a deep, deep knowing of the responsibility one takes when a trigger is pulled. Irreversible consequences usually occur at that point in time. I learned that day to respect the game I was harvesting, to take its life as cleanly as I possibly can, that no creature suffers needlessly. . . . That day in October, 1969, I was awakened. A part of me that did not exist was born.[4]

Football and hunting bring out something primal within us; something about the fall atmosphere makes many people feel energized and athletic, suddenly ready to go toss a football or take a hunting weekend in the mountains. But even those of us who do not play sports or enjoy hunting feel a heightened connection to the natural world at this time of year. We feel the need to be outside, to do something active and proactive.

But as fall shifts toward winter, the opposite can occur. The middle of the NFL season coincides with the often stormy weather of late autumn and provides a compelling excuse to stay inside. As one woman complained,

Tell me if this sounds familiar: it's a snowy, Sunday afternoon. A foot of fresh powder is glistening outside, calling your name to come out skiing. You get excited and actually start walking down the hall to find your husband when you stop. Almost as suddenly as the thought of going out occurs, your heart sinks and you turn back around. It's Sunday. During football season. If you're going out anywhere, you're going out alone. Your husband is currently sequestered in the living room with his nachos and PBR, watching the Bears. He won't be coming out anytime soon.

You narrow your eyes, silently cursing the National Football League. Thanks to them, you have even less time with your significant other. Thanks to them, there's now football on all day Sunday, Monday night, Thursday, and Saturday. You sigh, wondering if it would be worth it to just stop paying the cable bill and see what happened. Do sports addicts go through withdrawal symptoms?[5]

Football may not break up marriages, and for most people it's not an addiction, but it is a convenient reason to spend another cold and rainy November afternoon on the couch. This is not a minor thing. According to the Nielsen Company, more than one hundred million viewers watched Super Bowl XLIV in February 2010 (Saints 31, Colts 17).[6] In fact, Nielsen noted, a snowstorm that weekend "kept many viewers inside their homes, leading to impressive ratings in Washington, D.C." So seasonal weather impacts our sports watching, and sports impact our appreciation of the seasons, whether they bring us out on a fall morning or keep us inside on a chilly afternoon.

The Final Deadline: Year's End

In the deep phase of autumn, the pace of life quickens. We begin to realize the results of the increased enterprise that fall brings for many of us. Just as farmers gather the harvest so, too, do we start to bring in the goods. But many of us find it difficult to feel any satisfaction with our efforts. We often set false deadlines for ourselves: the big sale must be closed; the paper must be written; the project completed; the trip taken—all by a certain date. But, really, the deadline is self-imposed, a date we ourselves have entered on our own emotional calendars.

So, by mid-fall (just as Thanksgiving rolls around), many of my patients are feeling anxious. The sense of determination and energetic endeavor they felt in September has given way to a sense that the work isn't going as well as they had expected, or that they've hit snags and complications, or that they will not be able to meet those deadlines by the time the holidays arrive. Suddenly it seems as if everything has to be wrapped up by the end of the year, and it feels like an entire year's work gets concentrated into the weeks between Thanksgiving and December 31.

This is when people's behavior may change. They may start to look for help to keep them going. They turn to caffeine or alcohol; exercise fanatically or let physical activity slide; work constantly or find it hard to return to the office at the end of the weekend; seek help from prescription medicines. Awareness of how the season is affecting you becomes key but, as is usually the case, awareness is doubly difficult when you are feeling anxious. As a result, many people begin to feel exhausted. They become more passive. They take their foot off the gas. This, in turn, dispirits them and can push them farther along the negative path.

As fall moves into the waning phase and winter approaches, many of us try—just as we did at the end of summer—to deny that the season is coming to an end. We push harder, work harder. One young man I know continues to wear shorts and sandals, even as the wind turns sharp and everyone else has broken out their winter coats.

This is also the time, however, when many of my patients make a wonderful adjustment. They fully embrace the season. They accept a physical slowing down and create their own warm glow. They light a fire or a candle, stir up hot drinks, layer on the heavier clothing, and rejoice in the traditional colors of the upcoming holidays. Some make a point of going outside and experiencing the change of temperature and sunlight. Others prefer to spend more time inside and make their dwellings cozy and welcoming.

But some people cannot or don't want to adjust. They deny that the waning of the season has any effect on them. They want to keep on going as usual, whatever "usual" means to them. They become machinelike, following their routines rigidly. They are not aware that their productivity is waning along with the season and that their emotional calendar is out of sync with the natural one. This behavior is understandable in its seduction but is ultimately unrealistic. To try to sustain a nothing-can-get-me attitude is to create an unfair and false expectation of oneself that will inevitably lead to a sense of disappointment.

Simon: Hitting Bottom

As the trees go bare and nightfall comes earlier every day, thoughts of death and gloom readily come to mind for many people. Yet the darkening days simultaneously carry a sense of anticipation and energy. The holidays are approaching.

Come fall, one of my patients, Simon, suffers a fairly acute reaction to the loss of daylight and the prospect of all those approaching holidays. He is a founding partner and executive vice president of a large company. He travels all over the world for business—to offices in Hong Kong and Shanghai; shows in Paris; factories in Vietnam, Cambodia, and Bangladesh. He first came to see me following his divorce, which was brutal and emotionally draining for him, his ex-wife, and their two kids. Simon blames his ex-wife for many of the problems in his life.

Simon is Jewish, and when he was growing up, his favorite time of year was fall and early winter because of the High Holidays and Hanukkah. Several of his family members also had birthdays around this time, and he remembers the whole season as "Temple, temple, temple. Fun, fun, fun." As he grew older, many of his older relatives passed away—his grandmother died on Yom Kippur—leaving the family with fewer and fewer people joining them at the table. Eventually his family stopped celebrating the holidays altogether. His father just couldn't handle it.

So when they were first married Simon looked forward to starting a family with his wife, and he imagined how much fun it would be to spend the holidays again with his extended family. Simon's wife, however, did not share his interest in rekindling his joyful connection to the holiday traditions of Judaism. Quite the contrary. Not long after they were married, she found her way to Buddhism. As a result, the holiday season became even more stressful than it had been before. Simon and his wife had a difficult time deciding when and where to spend the holidays. Neither one wanted to slight his or her own family or miss any of the religious rituals; both wanted to have it their own way. "It was like her side always won," Simon remembers. "But it was so angsty." It got more and more difficult to resolve their conflicts and, at last, the marriage crumbled.

One might have hoped that the divorce would have solved Simon's holiday problem. Not so. The holidays still make life difficult for him. Now he feels lonely and bitter during this time of year. To make matters worse, he still fights with his ex-wife, but the battle now is over who will have the children with them at what times. "Being alone makes it doubly depressing," he admits. What, so long ago, was a joyful and spiritual time for Simon has become a time for dark thoughts, angry memories, and, all too often, self-pity.

Hanukkah is the lowest point in Simon's calendar. Even so, he hasn't given up on the ceremonies. Wherever he is in the world, he always lights the candles, symbols of hope for people all over the world.

But from then on through the end of January, according to Simon, "life sucks." Thankfully, however, Simon was aware of how deeply the season was affecting him, and he wanted to do something to change it. He grew tired of simply accepting that he would be miserable for months on end. He came to see me three years after his divorce, when he realized that as much as he wanted to change his situation he didn't know how to do it alone.

Simon's progress in treatment with me has relieved him of much of his traditional fall burden. Even though he knew why he was feeling upset, his awareness didn't automatically free him of his conditioning. It did help to talk about it. "It hasn't always been this way," he'd tell me, and we'd reach way back and talk about his happiest memories of the holidays and discuss ways he might recapture some of those warm feelings in a way that would suit his current life stage.

"I'd like to be able to let go of these unpleasant reminders," he said when he realized that he was falling back into his autumn funk. We worked together to release much of his emotional distress. We formulated a plan that included a combination of antidepressants and psychotherapy. After Simon began to feel refreshed, we considered his options and worked at constructing his future experience of the fall.

"It's not the same anymore," he said at a recent session. "I'm doing what I want now." Simon recently started a new company, relocated from the suburban coast to a city, and is enjoying his own traditions for the season.

One more thing about the fall: officially, it extends into

the season that we experience as winter—all the way to December 21, the shortest day of the year. So the waning phase of fall actually immerses us in the experience of winter. By the time winter actually comes, the days are already starting to get a little longer. As one of my patients with severe SAD once told me, "December twenty-second is really one of the best days of the year for me, even though I'm usually miserable."

"Because . . . ?" I prompted her.

"Because it's got one minute more sunlight than the day before," she said with a smile. "And from then on, time's working in my favor again!"

As fraught a time as autumn may be, then, at least it can end on a note of hope. Make the effort to plan ahead for the fall, especially for the latter part. Early fall is mostly about the alignment of energy. Once the transition out of summer is completed, fall can be a purposeful and productive time, but the end of the season requires redoubling your commitment and reviewing your plan on how to proceed. Ask yourself, How am I likely to be feeling as fall deepens? And come up with a few good ideas to help yourself along the way into winter.

4

The Wide Hand of Winter

It shows up, the winter. Splendid dictation

bestowed on me by slow leaves

suited up in silence and yellow.

I'm a book of snow,

a wide hand, a prairie,

an expectant circumference,

I pertain to earth and its winter.

—PABLO NERUDA, "Winter Garden"

WINTER IS A complicated time for me, as it is for many people. I'm a New England boy, yes, but I now maintain psychiatric practices and professional positions on both coasts, so I regularly travel back and forth between Boston and Los Angeles. I may leave Logan Airport while a snowstorm is gathering and touch down at LAX in near-80-degree balminess. I've gotten used to it, but the constant shifting from one mode to another can be both physically and emotionally wearing. My wife much prefers to extend her stays in one place or the other, rather than making shorter, more frequent trips. (My daughters are both in college now, so their lives are not so disrupted by my peregrinations.)

People have strong feelings about winter. Some focus on the hopeful and happy bustle that comes along with the holidays, while others dwell more on the gloominess of winter's cold and dark. One of the members of my research team happened upon a blog on the *New York Times* Web site in which readers posted their thoughts about winter and depression. What's interesting to me is how many people really love the characteristics of winter. These are just a few snippets to give you a sense of their feelings.[1]

> "I love the darkness, though I get the urge to sleep more, hibernate perhaps."
>
> "I think it's the quality of the light that attracts me. With the sun so far to the south, there are such long golden shadows on clear days. I also love the rain and wind. I just find this time of year exciting and a good time to take a look at myself."
>
> "I wait all year for the cold, dark weather. The quality of the light is gorgeous, and the fact that there's not much of it gives me permission to stay inside, read good books and decompress."

My friend Marie, the high-powered real estate executive, is one of those who find beauty in winter. For example, she notices how snow quiets people down. "I love a winter's day like that," she says. "I can't give myself a break to rest, but the snow will do it for me." The rain has the same effect on her. "It'll quiet me down. I don't have to meditate or pray or exhaust myself to be quieted down because the atmosphere is doing it for me."

Although many of us love winter, it can still be an emotional struggle, full of contrasts—joyous holidays and dark days, excitement and exhaustion, relief or regret at the ending of the year—combined with the commotion of year-end festivities set in the context of the seeming emptiness and isolation of midwinter. People often set unrealistic expectations for themselves and those around them throughout the holiday season. Many patients tell me they want to "wrap things up" but can't. The end of the year is approaching and the to-do list is still very long.

The emotional complexities are accompanied by the physical challenges that winter brings. Our lymphatic organs, which help us deal with disease, fluctuate in size all year but reach their largest in late autumn to early winter. The increased size indicates that the body has enhanced its immune functions, preparing to ward off attacks by bacteria, viruses, allergens, and any other foreign bodies that could potentially harm us. Keeping our bodies at a heightened state of readiness takes a great deal of energy, and some studies have shown that the decreased sunlight in winter makes it harder for the body to maintain enough energy to keep up its defenses to that degree, leading to compromised immune functions.[2]

Our hormone levels also fluctuate during the winter, which can affect the sex drive and make people feel sexually off-balance in the winter. Some feel a reduced interest in sex while others experience sharp ups and downs in their interest, far more so than they experience at other times of the year.

Brian: A Double Whammy

One patient of mine, Brian, has very real and ongoing problems with winter.

When we first starting working together, ten years ago,

Brian was not in good shape, experiencing one of his frequent bouts of depression. He was working as a band manager and traveling the world, setting up and running shows for a high-profile rock band, working extremely long hours in a high-pressure—and, let's face it, pretty unnatural—environment. Brian was good at his job and had helped build the band into a worldwide sensation. One of his clever practices was to book the band into venues during the off-season, when there was little competition from other acts. "I would have them tour cold places in the winter," Brian says, "when every band hates to go. I made them go to Arizona and Florida in the summer. It would be the only entertainment coming to town."

But what was good for the band was not so great for Brian. "For the band, having thirty thousand or forty thousand people yelling your name was an adrenaline rush," he remembers. "They'd really get it going. But there weren't thirty thousand people calling my name." So Brian, who has struggled with depression for all of his adult life, fell into severe episodes while on tour, and they were especially bad when he found himself in environments such as Norway or Sweden in the winter, where the days were short (sometimes the dark would stretch to twenty-two hours a "day") and temperatures could drop below zero. "I remember being in Sweden and going into a horrible depression," Brian recalls. "I'd think, 'I'm on tour in Europe and I want to slice my wrists!' Not really, but you know, I'd feel like I could barely get out of bed."

Being on tour was difficult enough, but Brian found that ending a tour could be even worse. As manic as the work might be, at least it kept him completely occupied and focused on the tasks that needed to be completed. When a tour was over, he suddenly found himself with too much time on his hands. The contrast was tough to deal with. In fact, he found these post-tour periods so difficult to manage that he turned to alcohol and drugs, particularly cocaine and speed, to self-medicate.

As it is for so many other people, the holiday season, from Christmas to New Year's, threw everything into overdrive, and Brian found it impossible to enjoy the holidays with his family. "I've tried it every which way. Having Christmas at my house, having Christmas at their house, having Christmas at my summer home. Just going to Christmas for an hour or two." None of these configurations worked. "Every time I would go into these horrible funks."

Brian's answer to this holiday hotspot was the same as it was to his on-tour stress and post-tour funks: self-medication through drug and alcohol abuse. "My alcoholism would just exacerbate and get out of control. I was a binge alcoholic. I wasn't constantly drunk, but I would be during that time of the year."

It all came to a head twenty-four years ago, on January 2, a day that is the hottest of hotspots on Brian's emotional calendar. That was the day he finally faced up to the fact that his lifestyle was a mess and he had to do something about his alcohol dependency. He joined Alcoholics Anonymous (AA) and began the long, hard work of getting and keeping sober—a job he still works at.

The timing is not unusual: the holidays can be a trigger for people who suffer with substance abuse problems, while the new year is a common time to take stock, realize that things must change, and then take some action in that direction. It's interesting to note, however, that no matter when the anniversary of joining AA may fall, it is a highly significant date for that person. "On that anniversary, people in AA start to get really squirrelly," Brian says. "It starts a couple of weeks before. And it's like clockwork for all of us."

Although resolving to get sober just after the holidays is

quite typical, the timing can complicate matters. "I get a double whammy: Christmas and my AA anniversary," says Brian. "Christmastime is just a really brutal time, so I go out of my way to be very gentle at that time, to surround myself with loving people."

Brian has been deeply changed by his participation in AA and, although I give him a lot of psychiatric help, he gets the most knowing and immediate support from other members of AA; that's fundamental to the way the program works. When Brian finds himself faced with an emotional challenge that he just can't manage on his own, he turns to a list of phone numbers of people in his AA community.

His alcoholism is under control now, but Brian still struggles with depression, particularly around Christmas and when he returns from business trips. But since renouncing alcohol, he has developed a new vice to fill the void brought on by his depression: overeating. In fact, that's one of the main issues that I have been helping Brian work through: instead of drinking when feeling empty or stressed out by his family, he began to eat enormous portions as a means of finding comfort. This, of course, serves to reinforce his holiday hotspots: there are few days in the year more filled with food than Thanksgiving, Christmas, and New Year's Eve. Brian has had to learn to apply the same strategies of restraint to his diet that have helped him to manage his alcoholism. As with his addiction, it is a constant struggle to choose the right path. Not long ago he called me after a particularly difficult episode. He was driving home from a post-Christmas visit to his sister (never an easy undertaking) and had stopped to tend his wounds at a roadside restaurant. He resisted the comfort food he so sorely craved. But by not overeating, he felt deprived, instead of better. So we took a closer look at his reactions: how he feels when hurt like this, and what he chooses to do next.

"It doesn't feel like a choice," Brian said. "I can't control how I feel." But by talking it through, I helped him understand that his feelings had led him astray. He found that he could take pride in choosing to take better care of himself by resisting unhealthy temptation.

Brian has also incorporated practices of mindfulness into his daily life. He moved from urban New England to Arizona, where he can go for hikes in the mornings with roadrunners, coyotes, and the occasional bobcat. His daily schedule includes writing and meditation. He also gets regular massage, healing touch, and Reiki treatments.

Awareness of the many positive changes that he has made in his life helps to keep Brian optimistic, especially as he confronts his personal hotspots. He tries to conclude each day by returning to the tenth step of the twelve-step AA program: take a personal inventory. "I try not to go to bed angry or depressed. So I review my day. I may see that I'm a little down or upset about a friend of mine. Or, I ate a basket of rolls before dinner and then had an unhealthy dinner. That's not how I usually eat now. That's old behavior. And I can change that tomorrow."

Hotspots from Chilling Moments

My friend Marie believes that bad weather can bring people together, especially during severe storms. "Sometimes you get this connection with neighbors," she says. "People come over for dinner. People call and ask, 'Do you have extra candles?' All of a sudden there's this sense of taking care of your neighbor that twenty-four hours ago was nonexistent."

That's exactly what happened, big time, during New England's legendary Blizzard of '78. The "Storm of the Century," as the media like to call it, hit the Boston area on Monday, February 5, 1978. In a twenty-four-hour period, it dumped a record-breaking 23.6 inches of snow on the city. The storm affected most of New England and parts of New York, with snowfall reaching higher than three feet in some areas.

The storm crippled the entire region for days. Drivers abandoned their snowed-in vehicles on Route 128, the main highway around the city. Boston's public transit system shut down. The state issued a driving ban. People set up impromptu shelters everywhere. Fifty-four people died as a result of the storm. Some drowned at sea. Some suffered heart attacks. Some people, who waited out the storm in their idling cars, died of carbon monoxide poisoning. The cost of storm damage, emergency care, looting, and curtailed work hours has been estimated at more than a billion dollars.[3]

Rosalyn Simons of Hull, Massachusetts, remembers being evacuated from her coastal home by boat and eventually finding refuge at the local high school. "My aunt, uncle, and myself along with many other Hullonions were about to spend the next few days not knowing what was happening to our homes and friends. It seemed like there were thousands of us there. People were sleeping all over the place. . . . The whole week we just stood in lines waiting for food."[4]

Once the worst was over, however, and she got home again, Rosalyn's memories support Marie's observations about the sense of community fostered by winter storms. "The week was declared a legal holiday. After I was safely home I could really enjoy the weather. Everyone was out walking here and there, as you could not take your car out. Everyone was so friendly. You saw people out who you never even saw before. Everyone was sharing stories and pulling kids in their sleds. Everyone was smiling and just enjoying."[5]

Rosalyn's memories of the blizzard, which are essentially positive, are shared by many others. For example, Harold Crapo, of Acushnet, Massachusetts, writes, "As I sit now and reflect upon this storm, what I remember most is how the community came together and helped one another."[6] Gloria Proulx-Morrissette of Fall River remembers meeting her newlywed neighbors who had not ventured out of the house until the third day after the storm. The woman's young daughter remarked to them, "I've been outside playing and inside playing. You must be doing a lot of playing inside, 'cause you haven't been outside!"[7] In fact, people in Boston regularly refer to the phenomenon of the "blizzard baby"—a child conceived during the storm. Although data show that, in fact, births in Massachusetts actually dropped in mid-November, the requisite nine months later, people still like the idea. One such believer is a man named Jim Healy, whose daughter Lauren was born at just about the right time to have been conceived during the blizzard. "Like everybody else, we stayed home," Jim says, adding, a little coyly, "And did things."[8]

While the Blizzard of '78 storm was an adventure that people loved to talk about later, for some it was traumatic. "I have to say that my memories are terrible," Kim Moore of Hull recollects. "I miscarried my first child during the blizzard of '78. It was a frightening experience. I actually went outside right after the power went out and I saw this darkness creeping up the street (it was a full moon and because of the light you didn't need the streetlights). I thought to myself . . . what on earth is that? Then I heard it . . . it was the ocean!",[9] which was flooding the streets.

These dramatic weather events can easily end up as

significant hotspots on the emotional calendar. Although no storm in the past hundred years has approached the Blizzard of '78 in accumulation and impact, every New England winter can be a reminder of that one storm. For people who remain in the region, the tendency to compare storms of today with the Blizzard of '78 can serve to reduce anxiety and reassure one another that things aren't as bad as they were then. Others, however, find themselves unable to shake the long-term effects of the blizzard. As one woman wrote, "I used to love snow but no more."[10]

Winter Catharsis: Let It All Hang Out

In the deep phase of winter after the holidays, in January and early February, many people feel depleted and in need of renewal, and desperately want a change of routine.

That is just what late winter festivals such as Mardi Gras are for. Today, Mardi Gras, which falls between February 3 and March 9, is celebrated by millions of people throughout Europe, Latin America, and the Caribbean. Based on the Roman Catholic calendar of holy days, the celebration takes place in the days before Ash Wednesday, the day that marks the beginning of Lent, during which believers abstain from eating meat, eggs, dairy products, and fruit. The Tuesday before Ash Wednesday is known as "Fat Tuesday," because it's the last chance for merrymaking and overindulgence in food, drink, and pleasures of the flesh for quite some time.

The roots of Mardi Gras can likely be found in the ancient pagan holiday of Lupercalia, which honored the pagan god Lupercus. He was a god of fertility, agriculture, and pastoral shepherds and was honored in mid-February with feasting, drinking, and other carnal excesses. Today, Mardi Gras has grown into a billion-dollar industry, and "partiers around the whole world are asked to let it all hang out," as one pumped-up Web video blasts.[11] Floats, pageants, masked balls, and dancing in the streets mark the celebration in many parts of the world, most notably in New Orleans, Rio de Janeiro, Nice, and Quebec City. In New Orleans, the revelry comes to an abrupt halt at midnight on Fat Tuesday, when police begin to clear the streets. The season of "letting it all hang out" comes with a clearly defined endpoint. A sign of the cultural wisdom of our forebears!

Quirky Holidays Presage Spring

The waning phase of the winter, late February and March, can be one of the most bewildering times of year for many people. In most regions of the country, February is the coldest month of the year, and March is the snowiest. During this time, many of my patients are torn between a desire to recommit themselves to their goals and activities from the beginning of the year, and an urge to simply give up and ride out the winter, waiting for the boost they hope will come with spring.

For sports fans, the Super Bowl marks the end of the American football season. Even basketball and hockey fans will admit that the sports landscape is different without football. The somewhat barren stretch until baseball begins goes right through the wintertime.

On February 2, Groundhog Day, we have to deal with the odd notion that a groundhog may be able to predict how long our wintry woes (or delights) are likely to last this year. As much as we dismiss the idea, it's hard not to hope that Punxsutawney Phil (or his backup groundhog, Pete) will give SAD sufferers a ray of hope.

Valentine's Day, however, a holiday that seems far more

commercial than traditional, brings on significantly more anxiety than does the emergence of the groundhog. For those in relationships, it can be a time of heightened expectations and pressure, while people without significant others face feelings of loneliness, no matter how much they turn up their noses at what seems to be a fabricated holiday.

"Valentine's Day: Hate it. Hate it," says Simon, who has been divorced for six years. "Nothing's ever gone right on that day, ever in my life. Ever." In fact, it's interesting that Simon's mood starts to pick up soon after Valentine's Day has passed. "Here's what's weird," he observes. "Right after the rains in California, right after Valentine's Day and through March, the Spanish broom, which is this amazing wildflower that makes the mountains look like they're on fire, starts coming up. And as soon as we see the first one, my son and my daughter and I stop to smell it. As soon as I see my first Spanish broom, it's going to be good."

There's a date that must surely be marked on Simon's emotional calendar: first bloom of broom. Life turns sweet.

In winter, you can try to keep on track with the plans you (hopefully) made in the late fall. Whether you are getting cozy and staying in more or bundling up and getting out, find something that makes sense for you. Enjoy what you can of what the winter offers—a lot or even just a little.

5

Spring: What *Do* You Want?

The frost was working out of the ground, and out of the
air, too, and it was getting closer and closer onto
barefoot time every day; and next it would be marble
time, and next mumbletypeg, and next tops and hoops,
and next kites, and then right away it would be summer
and going in a-swimming. It just makes a boy homesick
to look ahead like that and see how far off summer is.
Yes, and it sets him to sighing and saddening around,
and there's something the matter with him, and he don't
know what. . . . Don't you know what that is? It's spring
fever. That is what the name of it is. And when you've
got it, you want—oh, you don't quite know what it is you
DO want, but it just fairly makes your heart ache, you
want it so! It seems to you that mainly what you want is
to get away; get away from the same old tedious things
you're so used to seeing and so tired of, and set
something new.

—MARK TWAIN, *Tom Sawyer, Detective*

L ET'S START WITH the spring fever issue, since we'll have to come to it eventually.

To look at Mark Twain's photo today, with all that spiky hair and rather dour expression, you might not think of him as the popularizer of the term "spring fever," but, in fact, we do have him to thank for the widespread use of that expression. And we must also thank narrator Huck Finn for his eloquent description of just how most of us often feel at some point in spring: there is something you want, so urgently that it makes your heart ache, but you're not quite sure just exactly what it is. And, although Twain didn't say this, the not-knowing makes the heartache even more intense.

After all, nature is busily awakening and producing: trees budding, sap running, birds nesting, bees and butterflies reemerging, sunlight increasing, the air warming up. Shouldn't we be doing the same, somehow or other? Perhaps that's why we have the urge to move, to be outside, to do something unexpected and wild, to change things, even if they don't really need changing.

The popular media still love the idea of spring fever. In 2009, a Chinese movie called *Spring Fever* premiered at the Cannes Film Festival. The more accurate translation of its original Mandarin title is *A Night Deeply Drunk on the Spring Breeze*. Steamy stuff! I haven't seen the movie but, according to the Cannes Web site, it tells a torrid story of jealousy, spying, and a love triangle (or maybe it's a quadrangle, I can't quite tell). All of this action plays out during a succession of drunken nights in spring. The characters, the Web site tells us, "are possessed by an exhilarating madness of the senses, a dangerous malady that leads the heart and head astray."[1]

Is It a Fever or a Scurvy?

Let's for a moment consider this so-called malady in scientific terms. Is there something actually going on with the human body that might give rise to such exhilarating madness? According to Alfred Jay Bollet, in his book *Plagues and Poxes: The Rise and Fall of Epidemic Disease*, the term "spring fever" may well have been used by American colonists to describe the symptoms of scurvy that probably came about from a lack of vitamin C.[2] Colonists typically came down with the disease in late winter or early spring, when supplies of stored vegetables and fruits, those excellent sources of the needed vitamin, had been diminished or depleted, and new crops were still months away from harvest. However, the symptoms of scurvy—paleness, weakening, listlessness, fatigue, internal bleeding—are hardly what we associate with energetic spring fever.

Bollet may be right about the origins of the term (and perhaps Mark Twain simply reinterpreted it for his own purposes, which wouldn't surprise me a bit), but what about the scientific basis for the kind of spring fever we now think of—the far more attractive phenomenon that involves extra energy, vitality, and plenty of sexual appetite? Michael Terman, an expert on biorhythms at New York–Presbyterian Hospital (and a colleague of mine), says that whatever the causes of the condition, there are a number of physical phenomena that seem to be associated with spring, including increases in heart rate, loss of appetite, and mood swings. According to Terman, spring fever is a real thing, even if it is not a definitive diagnostic category.[3]

We believe that some of what's going on inside the body during this time involves melatonin, a hormone that governs our sleep-wake cycles. The body secretes high levels of melatonin during wintertime, but come spring a light-sensitive tissue in the eye senses the increasing amount of daylight and sends a signal to the brain, which then reduces the secretion of melatonin. As the level drops, we become more wakeful and less inclined toward the human version of hibernation. At the same time, the level of another chemical, serotonin, rises in spring. Serotonin is believed to be a mood-elevating neurotransmitter and may be a cause of the energy boost and enthusiasm that can characterize spring fever. Of course, if you have read any of the literature on the causes of depression, and the role of serotonin and melatonin and how various medications act upon them, you know there is a great deal of debate and disagreement within the medical community about these issues.

We know that there are many contributing factors to developing clinical depression, including genetic vulnerability, early exposure to stress, personal resiliency, and availability of safety and support. We also know that integrated treatment—problem solving, interpersonal therapy of one sort or another, and medication—combine to offer the greatest results. Antidepressant medication, which increases the presence of serotonin and norepinephrine, or the "feel-good" chemicals in the brain, sets up a cascade of effects that eventually stimulate mood centers, causing regrowth and arborization of neurons. Brain cells that degenerated during the depression are replaced by new ones. In other words, it's complicated, but antidepressants, often in combination with other types of treatment, do work well for many people.

Regarding sex and spring, the evidence is quite baffling. David Lam, at the University of Michigan at Ann Arbor's Population Studies Center, reports that birthrates for humans in northern Europe typically rise to 10 percent above the average in March—meaning that the babies were conceived in June. Another study shows that levels of testosterone in men and luteinizing hormone (which triggers ovulation) in women peak at 20 percent above average in June.[4] However, a study conducted by Till Roenneberg of the University of Munich and Jurgen Aschoff of the Max Planck Institute in nearby Andechs shows that men produce the most and the heartiest sperm in early spring, not June.[5] No one seems to agree on whose hormones are doing what, and when, at least not enough to reach a clear conclusion about conception!

And yet other research shows that people tend to have less sex in spring! Elena Conis, who is a science writer and health consultant, states the perplexity of spring fever succinctly. She writes, "In fact, many of spring's effects on the human mind and body are seemingly contradictory. Hormones do a partial job of explaining the seasonal epidemic of impulsive, giddy and amorous behaviors observed as the memory of winter fades, but much about the season's influences remains mysterious."[6]

No wonder we can't figure out what we really want during spring. Even so, despite our physical and emotional turmoil, it seems that the impulse to get outside as winter fades away is a healthy one, especially emotionally. Matthew Keller, of the University of Colorado at Boulder, studied five hundred people in the United States and Canada and found that the more time people spend outside on a sunny spring day the better their mood.[7] Interestingly, however, the good mood from sunshine decreases during the hotter summer months. Not surprisingly, 72 degrees Fahrenheit, room temperature, is the optimal temperature for a good mood.

Now, just to confuse matters, some cultures interpret spring fever more along the lines of scurvy than giddiness. Germans, for example, talk about *Frühjahrsmüdigkeit* ("spring tiredness"), which is characterized by low energy and weariness, sensitivity to changes in the weather, dizziness, irritability, headaches, and aching joints. The syndrome is not fully understood, but the theory is that it, too, is related to hormone balance: as the body's reserves of serotonin increase with more daylight, and more endorphins, testosterone, and estrogen are released, the complicated new ebb and flow puts a strain on the body.

Russians, according to *Moscow Times* humor columnist Michele A. Berdy, believe that "all mental and physical processes go kerflooey in the spring."[8] She reports that a typical newspaper headline in Russia is "Spring Is Here—Open the Door to Illness!" Health problems that Russians equate with spring include hypertension, kidney infections, gastritis, inflammation of the gallbladder, eczema, psoriasis, and hay fever. Mental health and nervous system problems include melancholy, headaches, dizziness, and decreased capacity for work. For Russians, spring fever can explain the extreme behavior of politicians. Everything that is already bad gets even worse in the spring, the Russians say, from the behavior of skinheads to fiscal inflation.[9]

Maybe the Russians aren't so far off the mark. Deaths by suicide actually peak in spring, a time when stereotypically— and, as we've seen, science backs it up—people's moods improve. Howard Gabennesch, a psychologist at the University of Southern Indiana, has proposed a theory that it's actually the gap between promise and reality that may lie at the root of the problem for severely depressed, suicidal people during this season.[10] Spring comes with expectations of fresh starts and new growth, but what if that new beginning doesn't actually deliver? For people with self-destructive tendencies, this disappointment may trigger a new level of hopelessness that can lead to the final act of suicide.

Another take on why suicide rates rise in spring has been proposed by Norm Dinges, a professor of psychology at the University of Alaska at Anchorage. Dinges thinks that the energy uptick we experience in spring may give a suicidal person the charge needed to take his or her own life.

"In spring, a person's depression may go into partial remission, but it's still strong," Dinges warns. "One of the greatest danger times is when people are improving. That's when they may have the energy to act out a dormant suicide plan."[11]

Linda: One Careless Day Can Mark a Lifetime

One of my colleagues, Linda, experienced a life-changing event that transformed spring, which had been her favorite time of year, into a painful emotional hotspot.

She wrote up the story for me, so let's hear it in her own words.

The house where I grew up is surrounded by colorful azaleas. My magical feelings around spring and my May 10th birthday started early, because my father would tell me every year that "the flowers come out for your birthday." He linked this day with this bursting forth of spring—so that my birthday felt like something much larger than my own life.

The sharp turn came when I was twenty-six years old. I was worn out from my first year in a Ph.D. program and went away for my birthday weekend to an island off New York with my fiancé and two friends. We decided after lunch to take a long walk to another part of the island that is miles away along the beach and through a forest. It was a picture-perfect spring day: sunny, not too hot, a light breeze.

I set out wearing only shorts and sandals. I noticed

along the way in the forest there were signs warning about Lyme disease, a tick-borne illness, but at the time no one knew much about it. All I knew about Lyme was that it could be cured with antibiotics. When we got to our destination we learned there were no water taxis to take us back as we'd planned, because it was off-season. We had to walk back. I was already exhausted—and now faced another four miles to get home. As we went back through the forest I remember shrubs and branches thwacking me. I was too tired to push things out of my way.

About six weeks later I began having dizzy spells. Over the next couple of weeks I fell very ill. I had stomach cramps, weird headaches, and body aches. I had no energy at all. I went to several doctors who diagnosed the "summer blahs." I started graduate school again but was a mess and could hardly get through class. Finally, a doctor friend suggested I get tested for Lyme disease. The result came back positive, but it had been in my system already for four months.

I was sick for several years. I finished my Ph.D. but gave up on my dream—which had been to be a professor. I couldn't handle the physical strains of an intense job. Managing a chronic illness is a daily discipline that still takes a lot of my time.

When my birthday comes around, I am always in a state of sadness and agitation. My birthday brings up memories of that day that changed my life: I often see and can even feel myself on the deck at the beach house making the decision to take that stupid walk. I count the years since I was in perfect health, and while each year I become stronger, I realize how long it's been since

I didn't have to think about my health every day. But worse than that, my birthday reminds me of my terrible carelessness and ruin of myself. I was careless not to take more seriously what could harm me. So it brings up a bad memory, and also reminds me viscerally of something that is painful to realize about myself.

For Linda, the month of May—which once signified flowers and self-celebration—now sets off powerful feelings of self-blame and regret. These are intrusive thoughts that can be hard to control. But Linda says that understanding her emotional calendar has already helped her recognize that spring, especially her birthday, are annual triggers for her—and this realization is helping her to manage those triggers.

Also, she's been able to embrace with new awareness some of the other parts of the season that bring satisfaction: "May tenth turns out to be the last day of frost in New England," she says. "That's a huge day for any gardener. I try to always get out and plant on my birthday. It brings me joy to be creating something, and I always pat myself on the back for getting out there even though I know there are ticks. I feel more vital when I face my fear down."

Allergies: The Real Itch of Spring

Linda's spring hotspot is an unusual one, but many people dread the coming of spring because they know they will have to deal with allergies. Seasonal allergies often correlate with rising temperatures and time spent outdoors, and can have a debilitating impact on daily life, causing sneezing, coughing, itching, sniffing, fatigue, lethargy, and depression.

Allergies occur when the body mistakes an allergen (such

as pollen, dust, or food) for a pathogen (something that causes illness, such as a bacteria or a virus). This causes the body to produce IgE antibodies—special proteins that in a healthy body are used to fight parasitic worms.

The first, or sensitizing, exposure to an allergen prepares the body for battle. The next time your system encounters the allergen, it goes into overdrive. The allergen triggers an immune response. Your immune system produces large quantities of protective compounds, such as histamine (hence the term "antihistamine"). This immune response can cause the runny nose, watery eyes, and mild wheezing associated with allergies. If the immune response is located in the tissues, it can cause hives. If it is located in the respiratory passage, it can cause asthma.

In people with severe allergies, the immune response can cause blood vessels to dilate so much that the person loses consciousness. Smooth muscle contractions can induce vomiting and diarrhea and cause airways to close. This reaction is known as anaphylactic shock and is most commonly caused by bee sting and nut allergies. People who know they are prone to anaphylactic reactions can prepare themselves by carrying an EpiPen, a syringe filled with epinephrine, that will clear their airways after a reaction.

Spring allergies are usually caused by tree pollen from oak, elm, birch, or other species. In summer, the culprits tend to be grasses and weeds. In fall, the instigator is usually ragweed. Hay fever, the most common seasonal allergy, is actually a misnomer because it has nothing to do with hay and is never accompanied by fever. It can occur in spring, summer, or fall, as different plants blossom.

In a blog about coping with mental illness, Jennifer Forbes asks, "I've had a ragweed allergy every August and September for the last few years. . . . I do take an antihistamine to prevent the sneezing, etc. However, I am having difficulty with the fatigue-lethargy-malaise combo. Many of you with allergies know what I'm talking about. How do you cope?"[12]

Jennifer is describing a dimension of allergies, emotional malaise, that is less familiar than the itching and sneezing, but recent studies show that there may well be a correlation between allergies and depression.

One of my patients, a corporate attorney in her midforties, originally came to see me because her spring allergies were so severe that she felt unable to enjoy her life. Every year she was caught feeling tired and headachey when others felt enlivened by the sun and warmth. At our first session together, she told me she had come because she was upset over not feeling the way she was "supposed to feel."

"It's such a happy time of year," she mused, "but not for me." She felt isolated from her friends during the spring each year. She spent less time with them deliberately, because seeing their good mood only made her feel worse—and she felt that she was dragging them down. "People who don't get allergic have no idea," she said.

While studies have been unable to conclusively identify where the association comes from, there does seem to be evidence of a link between allergies and depression. Some scientists believe that allergic reactions might release hormones that are associated with such mental health disturbances as weakness, malaise, depressed activity, hypersomnia, and apathy.[13] Others think that depression may increase the risk of having allergies, or that allergies and depression might share a common risk factor. While this link is uncertain, it seems clear that mental fatigue can appear alongside other more traditional symptoms of seasonal allergies.

What this means is that anyone with seasonally linked

allergies is liable to have a tough time come spring. Yet this fairly predictable seasonality seems to come as a surprise for many of my patients. Time and time again, allergy sufferers forget for a while what is in store for them when spring arrives. And until their awareness kicks in, there can be an awful period of feeling off and not knowing why. "What's wrong with me?" they ask. "How come I'm not myself?" The physical aspects of allergies are difficult enough; by making sure you're aware that they're a hotspot on your calendar, you can stave off the worst of the emotional impact.

Spring Holidays: After Groundhogs Come Bunnies?

Culturally, at least in this country, spring can be an emotionally fraught time (as every season can be!), what with tax season, Easter, spring break, the end of the school year, Mother's Day, and Memorial Day.

For Marie, spring reminds her of the fact that she does not have children and that she probably never will. "When you're not in school or you don't have school-age children, you're out of sync," she says. "You're just out of sync."

Tax season, that dreaded yearly assessment of income, expenses, dependents, and losses, causes many to wonder about the turns their lives have taken. Feelings of inadequacy and general malaise are common at this time.

Several Jewish colleagues have told me that while they look forward to Passover's family rituals and meals, Easter—historically the peak time of anti-Semitic violence or pogroms in eastern Europe—can be an unsettling time for them. Jesus's Last Supper was a Passover Seder, so the two holidays are inextricably linked on the Judeo-Christian calendar.

Memorial Day, the day set aside to honor those who gave their lives in America's service, can be a difficult one for many. Memories of friends and family members lost, and reflections on how the United States has participated on the world stage, can bring us joy or sorrow, and often both.

For kids in spring, childhood expert Terri Mauro notes, "long days of rain and the lack of outdoor play that [spring] brings can make kids feel antsy, and staring out a classroom window at a beautiful sunny day can make them restless."[14] Allergies and the lightheaded, disoriented feeling that also comes with them make it difficult for kids to focus. In the waning phase of spring, during the end-of-school period, frenzied energy and worry also affect parents, and many adults experience tension due to remembered stress from their school days.

Mauro advises that we all slow down during this time—and with that awareness, I'd add, will come seasonal embrace. "If you're suffering from allergies," she writes, "feeling the changes in weather, going crazy with closet changes, agonizing over the way your spring clothes fit, getting caught up in vacation plans, worrying about what to do with your child over spring break, all of these things will up your stress level and lower your levels of patience, understanding, and time to spend with kids. . . . Stop and take a look at whether your stress may be contagious. And then smell the flowers. Help your child smell them, too."[15]

When You Don't Have It, You Miss It

As tricky as spring may be to deal with, those who have grown up in a climate where there are distinct seasons miss them when they move someplace where the seasons unfold differently. Expatriates in tropical climates report that they experience the lack of a winter-into-spring cycle in surprisingly powerful ways.

Canadian copy editor Andrew Raven, who lives in Singapore, writes that he feels left out of the spring fever buzz that he remembers from northern climes: in Singapore, where the seasons are "monochromatic," he "can't shake the nagging feeling that something is just a little off."[16] He goes on:

"This is a time of year when Canadians, Americans, Swedes, Finns and their northern brethren are bombarded with natural cues that signal the end of a long winter. The days grow longer. Leaves sprout from the grey frames of trees. And dog poop long since buried under the snow begins to reemerge. All that renewal engenders in most Northerners a sense of optimism.

"It is a psychological boost that I miss in Singapore," he realizes, "where one day is a mirror image of the last (as beautiful as they might be)."[17]

Sure, there were no seasons in the original Garden of Eden. But in the real world most of us rely on seasons to—among other things—mark phases of emotional change. We crave spring to "get away from the same old tedious things . . . and set something new."

Try to harness the restive energy that spring brings. You can feel it: put it to use for yourself. Ask yourself, What springtime celebration can I plan? It doesn't have to be elaborate or logistically complicated. How about something simple to honor or "tip your hat" to what's in store? I, for example, might put on a more brightly colored tie, or bow tie, and walk through the Boston Public Garden rather than take a taxi around it, looking at the very beginning of nature's season of renewal.

PART II

The Environmental Factors

A change in the weather is sufficient to
re-create the world and ourselves.

—MARCEL PROUST, *Remembrance of Things Past*

In Jane Austen's book *Pride and Prejudice*, Jane Bennet's life is put at risk by a rainstorm. Jane's mother, in fact, is the one who jeopardizes her daughter's safety, by deliberately sending her out without a carriage to travel, on horseback, to a neighbor's stately home. There, her mother hopes, Jane will be stranded with the wealthy and eligible Mr. Bingley for the duration of an impending storm. Instead, Jane gets caught in the deluge and becomes feverish at his estate. In the nineteenth century, when the story takes place, people were constantly exposed to ailments related to the environment, such as chilblains, trench foot, rickets, and, of course, the common cold. All ends well, however, because Jane and Mr. Bingley do indeed fall in love, as do her sister Elizabeth and Bingley's friend Mr. Darcy, who also happens to be at Mr. Bingley's estate.

Today, we can choose to limit our exposure to the weather. In developed countries, we have transportation systems that provide much more cover than the average horse. We have weatherproof clothing. We enjoy heating and cooling systems that, depending on their effectiveness, can keep our environments at close to the optimal 72 degrees Fahrenheit. Our health care system, even with all its failings, helps us prevent, control, and cure many diseases. And if the environment becomes completely intolerable, we can always hop in a car, board a train or a plane, or commandeer a boat and simply remove ourselves to some other place where the physical conditions are more to our liking: someplace warmer or colder or more or less temperate. We are much less likely to suffer from chilblains as the result of a three-mile journey on horseback to visit a neighbor.

And yet we are not as disconnected from the external environment as we may think. Just because we no longer have to travel by foot along muddy roads in the spring doesn't mean we're not impacted by rain, which can inflame joints and impact serotonin levels. Just because we don't rise with the sun doesn't mean we don't feel the effect of decreased daylight in winter and increased light in summer. And although we have infrastructure in place to protect us, there are still weather events that can halt the smooth running of even the most sophisticated of cities and disrupt our lives in violent and unpredictable ways.

But it does not take a tsunami or an earthquake to throw us off balance. The most fundamental of environmental conditions can affect our physical and emotional well-being: in particular, light, temperature, and wind.

If you disregard them, as Jane Bennet did, you put yourself in one or more kinds of peril.

Steve: Trying to Live Beyond the Body

That is precisely what happened to Steve. He's not a patient of mine, but I wish he had been. Working together, we might have been able to prevent the devastating physical meltdown he suffered at the age of forty-three.

By most outward appearances, Steve looked to be a man completely on top of his game. An international management consultant and author of several books on business strategy, Steve typically traveled 230 of the 250 workdays each year. Of course, that does not mean that Steve worked only on actual workdays. "One of the interesting things about being an international consultant," he says, "is that you can always find a holiday to work on." In the early 1980s, he was based in Japan, where his travel routine was especially grueling. He would spend ten days in Japan, fly to the United States for ten days, return to Japan for ten days, and then on to Europe for ten more days of work. Then he'd start the cycle all over again, for the six years he spent in Japan. Some of Steve's Japanese colleagues warned him that too many of these back-to-back-to-back-to-back trips would erode his health, but Steve said he found the fast pace thrilling.

Steve returned to the United States in 1985 and, although it sounds impossible, he picked up his pace of travel, sometimes flying to Japan and Europe in the same week. As a consultant who thrives on solving problems, and with a background in engineering, Steve enjoyed finding clever solutions to tricky meeting schedules in multiple cities. "I found a route through Moscow that allowed me to work in the afternoon in Japan and still come back to the U.S. at night," he says. "That's the kind of thing I would search out and find. My solution for Europe, at its most extreme, was the overnight flight. I'd have a meeting in Frankfurt, then take a nine o'clock flight out of London that could get me home on the same night. I'd sleep on the plane to Frankfurt, go to the meeting, and sleep on the plane coming back." For a period of ten years, Steve logged more than five hundred thousand miles per year in the air.

Given such an itinerary, you might think that Steve's performance would be negatively affected. But he says that it was not: he would be alert and ready to go as soon as he reached his destination. If he arrived in a city early in the morning, he would pop into one of the many airline clubs he belonged to for a quick shower and shave before catching a cab to his first meeting of the day. "The one-day trips were actually the easiest," he says. "Arrive in the morning, back at night. I was tired the next day, but I wasn't beat. The two- and three-day trips were the hardest. Getting over jet lag while I was there, getting over it when I came back. By the third day, I was kind of back on my feet. And feeling pretty good." He fueled himself with diet sodas, but "wasn't big" on taking any kind of sleep medication because he would wake up feeling groggy.

Steve has a family, and quite a large one at that—a wife and six kids. Keeping up such a hectic travel schedule made it particularly difficult to stay connected with them. But that may have actually suited his temperament. He found that taking care of the kids, especially when they were young, was far more difficult than devising new routes around the world. For a while, he took the 12:30 A.M.-to-dawn shift, on call for his young children while his wife got some sleep. "To me, that was far worse than jet lag," Steve says. Still, Steve took good advantage of those sleepless hours. In between responding to the needs of one or more children, he would work on his latest manuscript, filling up one pad after another with longhand.

The biggest issue Steve had with travel was keeping in contact with his wife while he was away. "If I'm in Europe, it's too early to talk to her before I go to work. After I come home from work, she's in the middle of her day. So I've got to talk to her at nine or ten o'clock at night, and I'm not in the mood to talk to anybody at nine or ten o'clock at night on these trips," he says.

Technology to the rescue. "The thing that probably saved my marriage was the BlackBerry. I had one of the very first ones," Steve says. "You had to call an operator and dictate a message, and it came over on a line item. But it freed us from having to play phone tag. It actually sustained communication throughout the course of a day, no matter where I was."

When Steve's kids got older, he tried another solution to familial disconnection: he brought his wife and kids along on some of his trips. Steve himself had traveled a lot when he was a kid. An armed services brat, he had moved with his family more than twenty times. "All my kids have traveled quite a bit. Not all of them like it, as it turns out," he says.

It was only a matter of time before Steve's globe-trotting caught up with him. When he turned forty-three he began to notice the first signs that everything was not right. "That's when I said, 'This is beginning to hurt.' Until then it didn't really bother me that much." It wasn't a milestone birthday, but it was the first time he noticed some cracks in his armor. "I said, 'I just can't keep doing this. It's a young man's game.' I was commuting to Japan again, and Europe, to a lesser extent. I noticed the days were just harder. When I got off the plane and went into these meetings I didn't feel like king of the hill. I felt tired. And I felt really terrible when I got home."

He remembered the advice from his Japanese colleagues to limit himself to ten major trips per year, but he had never heeded it. "I was doing fourteen or fifteen trips. I said, 'I can do it, guys. You're just a bunch of wussies.' Then, at forty-three, I said, '*I'm* a wussy now.'"

But what he felt was more than tiredness. While in Japan, he had developed a hacking cough. "I finally saw a couple of doctors about it. Their hypothesis was that my body was behaving as if it had a cold, possibly because of the air on the airplane. But there was no evidence my body had a cold. The doctors' recommendation was to stop flying, which at the time was impossible."

Yet the cough was trivial compared to the health problems to come. While in Thailand, he was stricken with hepatitis and then, on a trip to England, came down with pneumonia. Nevertheless, by 2003, he was working harder than ever. "It was a very intense work time. I was tired," he admits.

Now in his early fifties, Steve began seeking help from a psychologist. His condition was bad enough that his life insurance agent was in contact with the psychologist and told him that Steve had to change his lifestyle. "He said, 'You're going to kill yourself,'" Steve says. "But I didn't feel like I was dying."

His body felt otherwise. Steve was in New York when he began to feel terrible. His instinct was not to go to the hospital but to get on a plane and fly to Boston, where one of his firm's offices was located. He checked into a hotel room where he began to vomit blood. Again, he decided to get on a plane and fly home. When he arrived there, he had lost so much blood he was taken directly to the emergency room. They released him, but he got worse and was readmitted. He lingered and eventually fell into a coma that lasted for three months. He was pronounced dead three times.

What caused Steve's collapse? "The doctors have a long list of things," he says, "with stress being at the top of the list. Jet lag was behind that, because it's a driver of stress. I also had a condition with my blood vessels in which the walls were thinning. And that meant when they broke, they wouldn't heal," he says.

But even when Steve was taken off life support, he did not, in fact, die. As battered as his body was, it did not accept the final verdict. One day, almost miraculously, he sat up in bed and demanded to know where he was. At last, he got well enough to leave the hospital, but his life changed dramatically. He went on full-time disability leave for six months, during which he wasn't allowed to drive. He spent more time at his home, a "very peaceful" farm, than he had in years. But it would not be accurate to say that Steve spent all his time resting and tending to his health. He finished writing another book, and then went back to work part-time. Other remedies were simpler: "Reduce stress, don't travel as much, eat and drink intelligently, and exercise," Steve says. "And I take a ton of medicines. I must take twelve pills a day."

Now Steve is back on the road, but he does not push himself as hard as he used to. "My psychologist said, 'If you're going to travel, either go for one day or go for a week. Anything between, you're going to suffer.' He's right. Every time I've violated that rule I've paid a big price. It easily wipes me out for three or four days." Steve also tries not to work superlong days and tries to carve out an hour or two to rest or read. As for medications, he has found melatonin, which balances the sleep cycle, to work best with time zone effects. Once in a while, he will take a sleeping pill, but he still doesn't like them much. Steve also tries to do more teleconferencing and schedule trips only when necessary. "If someone asks, 'Can you be in Singapore?' I think about it before I say yes."

Overall, Steve tries to pace himself more carefully and does not try to beat the diurnal and nocturnal rhythms that make up normal human existence. "I've had a mortal experience. So I don't rush in and rush out when I travel. It's worth hanging around for a few days and experiencing these places. There are a lot of places I've been to in the world that I really never took the time to see, because I was just there to get something done. If you can see more, it's psychologically much more healthy."

When Steve is at home, what does he do to relax? He builds and flies radio-controlled airplanes, of course.

6

Running Cold and Hot

The heat was excessive; he had never suffered any thing
like it—almost wished he had staid at home—nothing
killed him like heat—he could bear any degree of cold,
etc., but heat was intolerable.

—Jane Austen, *Emma*

FORTUNATELY, VERY FEW of us are travelers on Steve's level. We do not subject ourselves to the incredible variations of climate, both environmental and cultural, that Steve did. I think it's safe to say that Steve's ailments were largely caused by overwork and stress, but it's hard to discount the effects of a constant barrage of fluctuating physical factors—light, temperature, and air quality—on his ability to maintain homeostasis.

Perhaps logging that many miles in a year makes one both less aware of these effects and more susceptible to them. I am exceptionally sensitive to the way environments can affect me physically and emotionally when I travel. I remember one summer when I flew from Nantucket to attend a psychiatric conference at an office park not far from Chicago's O'Hare International Airport. I woke up that morning in full summer mode, and the temperature rose to 80 degrees before I flew out. I arrived in Chicago in the early afternoon and went directly to a conference room that had been super air-conditioned. It must have been 68 degrees, but it felt like 50 to me. From the moment I touched down to the time I left forty-eight hours later, I was in that refrigerated condition. In one of the meetings, a colleague pulled the shade over the windows to project his PowerPoint presentation. I think I actually shivered. I looked around—nobody else seemed to mind. Perhaps they were used to it. I had to fight to stay focused and make a contribution to the meeting.

"Climate control," I thought to myself, "has its limits."

Cold and Its Adaptations

People have remarkably varied reactions to temperature. Some people cannot stand the heat, some cannot bear the cold, and, for some, moderately cold temperatures are less bearable than really freezing ones.

Of the two temperature extremes, cold seems to be more complex and, in many ways, more emotionally interesting than heat. Bill Streever's fascinating book *Cold: Adventures in the World's Frozen Places* captures much of this complexity, and we cite his work in several places in this chapter. Streever is one of those people who love the cold. "In my experience," he said in an NPR interview about his book, "cold helps you feel alive. You walk outside on a brisk day, and there's nothing like a breath of fresh air. Suddenly you're awake. It's better than coffee."[1]

Not all living creatures handle cold quite like Streever. Many, of course, simply die when the temperature drops, but a

wide variety of animals and insects—including birds, butterflies, and mammals—head south in the winter to escape the
cold. Many of us follow their lead. One of my patients, Gloria, a
resolute Bostonian, visits the Caribbean as often as she can.
LaDonna Bates, a remarkable woman who hates winter, also
heads for warm climes. I spend almost half my time in Los
Angeles, which allows me to regularly defrost from the New
England cold.

But those creatures that stay in the cold have developed
remarkable adaptive mechanisms that help them survive the
winter. Owls and wolves, for example, grow winter coats to add
insulation. Bears and other mammals hibernate. Chipmunks
hunker down for the winter with a store of easily accessible food
and take "catnaps," rather than going into full hibernation.[2]
The wood frog survives by flooding its blood with glucose and
freezing itself into an icy patch.[3]

Humans also have their management mechanisms, and gaining weight is the most common and effective. Although weight
gain is rarely seen as a good thing in our culture today, insulat-
ing fat can help the body cope with low temperatures. And the
increased activity of the digestive process, working overtime as
food consumption increases, creates warmth of its own. This
rise in metabolic rate means that people from populations that
live in extreme cold can burn 13 to 40 percent more calories
than individuals who live in warmer climates.[4] Polar explorers,
eating a meat- and blubber-filled diet to maintain energy levels,
easily consumed six thousand calories a day,[5] compared to the
two thousand that we now think of as normal.

The human body also has a specific homeostatic regulatory
system for cold. When exposed to cold, blood vessels contract
in a process called vasoconstriction, which is the opposite of
heat-induced vasodilation. This directs blood flow away from

extremities and toward the core, keeping the all-important organs, including the heart and lungs, as warm as possible. If this contraction of the blood vessels can't do the job, the body's core temperature begins to fall. When it drops below 97 degrees Fahrenheit, the hypothalamus, that thermostat of the brain, instructs the body to start another defense mechanism: shivering. This is nothing more than a rapid contraction of the muscles, but shivering very effectively produces heat—as much as four times more heat than the body produces when at rest.[6]

Babies are particularly sensitive to cold, because they are so small. So nature has provided them with special cells that keep them extra warm. These cells are contained in a brown adipose (fatty) tissue, unique to infants, that is found in the neck and chest regions. While most cells produce just a little bit of heat as a by-product of metabolic activity, brown adipose cells have no other purpose but to generate heat. Instead of storing energy, these cells break down fat and exude the resulting energy in the form of heat.[7]

UNHAPPY AND HAPPY RESPONSES TO COLD

Not everyone is equipped to handle the cold as well as newborn babies are.

One of the great cold-weather myths is that cold weather can make you sick. This leads to much bundling up of small children by protective parents and grandparents before they go out to play. The more scientifically minded believe, incorrectly, that the reason people get sick in the winter is because cold suppresses the immune system. One group of scientists, after finding that cold seemed to increase sickness rates in test subjects, suggested that perhaps it was because cold noses have less blood due to vasoconstriction.[8] Less blood means a less active immune system, making it easier for viruses in the nose to take hold, and for people to catch a cold.[9] But most scientists agree that as long as your core body temperature stays constant, your immune system does not change.[10]

If the body is exposed to too much cold, our homeostatic regulators will eventually fail. As blood vessels constrict to maintain the core body temperature, the extremities—hands, feet, noses, and ears—get frostbite, which means that they begin to freeze. When the core body temperature drops below normal, the body falls into a state of hypothermia. If the core of the body remains mildly hypothermic for long enough, it will eventually use up its store of glycogen and shivering will stop. Below 85 degrees Fahrenheit, the regulatory system managed by the hypothalamus stops functioning. Both of these scenarios result in severe hypothermia, and the processes keeping the body alive slow down. Finally, these processes will stop completely and the unfortunate person freezes to death.

And yet cold can also be a lifesaver. There's a saying in the medical field: "You're not dead until you're warm and dead."[11] That's because exposure to extreme cold can decrease heart and metabolic rates to the point of being barely discernible, and this can actually prolong life. Consider the remarkable story of Dr. Anna Bagenholm, a Swedish medical student, as reported in a story by CBS News. Bagenholm was skiing in Norway when she slipped headfirst under a waterfall and became trapped against the river's ice. She remained submerged for eighty minutes before medical rescuers were able to release her. When she was finally pulled from the water she had no pulse.

Nonetheless, medics began CPR, and Bagenholm was transported to a hospital in Tromsø where she was hooked up to a bypass system and her blood was slowly and carefully warmed. Nine hours later, her heart was once again beating on its own and her temperature was back to normal. Because the cold had slowed her metabolic rates, her brain needed very little oxygen to stay alive. Although she experienced nerve damage in her extremities, Bagenholm recovered from her near-drowning experience with no brain damage at all.[12]

Cold Defeats an Army

Cold does more than make us shiver or cause hypothermia. Its physical effects have emotional consequences, and the combination can lead to political and military disaster, as it did for French emperor Napoléon Bonaparte and his army in 1812.

In June of that year, Napoléon assembled an army of nearly five hundred thousand soldiers and began an attack on Russia with the intention of conquering the massive nation once and for all. Knowing and fearing Napoléon's reputation as a commander, the Russians wanted to avoid regular battle. Instead, under Field Marshal Mikhail Kutuzov, the Russians began to retreat from their European borders, devastating the land and destroying food, crops, and firewood as they went. As the French pressed forward through the bleak and ravaged landscape, the Russians employed guerrilla tactics to strike at small numbers at a time.

Early winter—which arrived in September in Russia that year—had a hugely destabilizing physiological effect on Napoléon. He caught cold, developed a persistent cough, and began to suffer from a chronic condition that often attacked him in the cold weather, called diuresis—an increased production of urine coupled with a decreased ability to urinate. This caused Napoléon intense discomfort and hampered his ability to concentrate and make decisions. As Philippe-Paul de Ségur, one of Napoléon's aides-de-camp, wrote in his famed diary *Defeat: Napoleon's Russian Campaign*, Napoléon "had been adversely affected by fatigue and the first signs of the equinox, and realized that at this critical moment his genius was chained down, as it were, by his body, overwhelmed by the triple weight of fatigue, fever, and an ailment [diuresis] which perhaps more than any other drains a man of physical and moral strength."[13]

Suffering constantly, Napoléon marched with his troops all the way to Moscow and, after a ferocious battle with the Russian army, occupied the capital city. However, a large army occupying even a major city cannot sustain itself for long without a massive supply chain, especially in the winter. By mid-October, Napoléon concluded that the occupation could not continue and ordered a retreat from Moscow. The army of a half million French soldiers marched across five hundred miles of forest and tundra, with dwindling food and medical supplies, the weather growing more severe by the day. The cold was so intense that the buttons on the soldiers' uniforms snapped.[14] Hundreds of thousands died from cold, starvation, and disease, and many more deserted the army or committed suicide out of depression and despair. By the time the French army reached friendly soil, only ten thousand soldiers remained. As Ségur wrote, "He had been overwhelmed by the Russian autumn!"[15]

Heat Sensitivity

Hot weather has its own ordeals, although they are generally not as life-threatening as the cold. In chapter 2, I introduced Jenny, who suffers in hot weather. Jenny described her feelings during the summer as a malaise, saying, "Physically, I feel really draggy, like I'm walking through Jell-O." I know exactly what she means: that combination of tiredness, weakness, and stickiness that occurs on a really hot day. But what causes this Jell-O sensation?

Heat sensitivity is all about homeostasis, the tendency of the body to maintain stable levels of water, glucose, salt, and heat that is managed by a human thermostat called the hypothalamus.

When we get hot, the human thermostat uses two major mechanisms to keep us at a comfortable 98.6 degrees Fahrenheit. Sweating, as we all know, is the excretion of water through pores in the skin. As we sweat, water evaporates off the skin in a chemical process that uses heat as an energy source. Evaporating water sucks heat from our skin, and we cool off. (Humidity slows down evaporation, which is why we feel even more uncomfortable on hot and humid days.) Sweating is paired with vasodilation, the expansion of blood vessels near the surface of the skin,[16] which allows maximum blood flow in that area and gives the blood a chance to cool down before it returns to the core of our body.[17]

Heat regulation comes at a price, however. Without vasodilation and sweating, we wouldn't be able to survive in hot summer temperatures. But sometimes our body doesn't respond well to these changes. Expanding blood vessels, combined with water loss, can lead to low blood pressure. This can cause heat edema, a swelling of the hands and feet that is especially likely to occur if you sit or stand in a hot place for a long time. It can also cause heat syncope, that blackout feeling you get sometimes when you stop moving after exercising on a hot day. Heat syncope occurs when a decrease in blood pressure causes less oxygen to reach your brain.[18]

Sweating can have negative effects, too. If your pores are blocked, your body's attempt to sweat can irritate your skin and cause heat rash, an uncomfortable irritation of the skin. Mild dehydration, a surprisingly common condition during the summer, can make you feel lethargic and weak, thirsty, and dizzy or light-headed—all symptoms of Jenny's summer malaise. Fortunately, many of these conditions can be treated by moving to a cool space, resting, and drinking cold beverages, like Jenny does when she goes to school events with a jug of ice water. Juice is an especially good beverage choice because it can help the body maintain homeostasis by providing both water and electrolytes.

Dehydration and Hyperthermia

The story of Mauro Prosperi, as reported in *Outside* magazine, is an amazing example of survival in the hottest of conditions. In 1994, Prosperi was running a marathon through the Moroccan Sahara when a sudden sandstorm obscured his vision and forced him off the trail. When the storm was over, Prosperi was alone and lost in the desert.

For days he wandered the desert, looking for a path. On the third day, he found himself at a deserted Muslim shrine, where he was able to get sustenance from the blood of two small bats he killed. Certain that his life was over, Prosperi wrote a note to his family with charcoal from the shrine and attempted to slit his wrists. But his blood had thickened so much from dehydration that it would not run.

After eight days in the desert, Prosperi encountered a group of Tuareg nomads who gave him water and brought him to a village. He was 130 miles west of his original course; he had lost thirty-three pounds, and his liver was severely damaged. But he made a full recovery—so much so that as of 2004, he had returned to Morocco to complete the marathon six times.[19]

Prosperi's survival is extraordinary in the face of the two deadliest risks that accompany extreme heat: severe dehydration and hyperthermia.

If mild dehydration isn't counteracted quickly, the body can progress to severe dehydration. Blood pressure can fall, causing orthostatic hypotension, which is a feeling of light-headedness or fainting when you stand up. As dehydration continues, the lack of water and low blood pressure lead to shock and severe damage to internal organs. Tissues begin to shrivel and cells begin to shrink and malfunction. Malfunctioning brain cells lead to confusion, which is one of the most telling signs of severe dehydration. Eventually, the body slips into a coma.[20]

As the body overheats, it can also become hyperthermic, a less familiar opposite to hypothermia. At some point as we get hotter, homeostatic regulation breaks down, and the body can no longer maintain homeostasis. Like its cold-weather counterpart, hyperthermia can have severe consequences.

As the body begins to overheat, muscles start to cramp, a symptom known as heat cramps. These cramps are followed by heat exhaustion, which looks a lot like dehydration, except that the skin gets damp and cool to the touch. Heat exhaustion eventually progresses to heatstroke, which occurs when your core body temperature surpasses 104 degrees Fahrenheit. At this point, the homeostatic regulatory systems shut down and you stop sweating. Your heart will start racing, your skin will be flushed, and you may lose basic cognitive function, begin seizing, have difficulty speaking, or lose consciousness. Heatstroke, like extreme dehydration, is a medical emergency and requires immediate clinical care.

The Cultural Response to Heat

Most of us don't encounter near-death heat experiences on a regular basis. Instead, we are more likely to be affected by the gentler symptoms of heat, such as mild dehydration and general discomfort. This is probably why so many hot-weather communities deal with the heat in a quiet way. Unlike cold weather, which seems to appeal to people's sense of adventure, heat is generally a lethargic experience. People go inside, take a nap, and wait for it to pass. The Spanish siesta is a beautiful example of a cultural adaptation to the heat.

But sometimes these relatively minor symptoms can have far-reaching effects. Researchers at Fudan University in Shanghai discovered that just a one-degree rise in temperature over three days led to a 37 percent increase in fatalities from various causes, from heart attack to stroke. Scientists have also blamed rises in temperature for increases in certain kinds of crime, and even rioting.[21] Given these conditions, napping seems like an excellent alternative!

7

∽

Living in Light and Dark

A sensible man will remember that the eyes may be
confused in two ways—by a change from light to
darkness or from darkness to light; and he will recog-
nize that the same thing happens to the soul.

—Plato, *The Republic*

"The whole world is energy," observes Marie. "Every-thing's buzzing, everything's ricocheting off everything else. There's a certain hum and buzz to life. And bright light seems to intensify that hum." Marie thinks of humans as running on natural battery packs. These battery packs, she believes, are solar powered.

Humans are indeed diurnal, or daylight, creatures. We wake more or less with the rising sun and go to sleep more or less when it gets dark. In contrast to owls, with their massive irises, or bats with echolocation, we have visual and other senses that are adapted to sunny living. Our production of melanin, the skin pig-ment that gives you that summer tan (be careful!) and serves as a natural sunblock, is one example of the way that our bodies have adapted to life in the sun. Another is the increased production of serotonin, the neurotransmitter that is believed to be associated with mood elevation, during the brightest times of day and the sunniest times of year.[1]

Life is closely attuned to the movement of the sun. Plants, animals, and humans alike have cells that register the sun and respond accordingly, managing everything from sleep hormones to sex drives. Plants have a "molecular hourglass" that measures the length of each day. When days become long enough, signaling spring, the plants burst into bloom.[2] Birds respond to increased day length during the spring by producing hormones that fire up their sex drives so that they can raise their chicks during the summer.[3] And we humans have a photosensitive gland in our brains that regulates our sleep cycles in response to sunlight. We are only beginning to understand the ways that our bodies react to sunlight over days and seasons, but it is a complex and profoundly significant process. It's no wonder that humans have been worshipping the sun for thousands of years.

Powered by the Sun

Let's talk about some of the benefits of living with the sun. Plants are able to channel the power of the sun to create food through photosynthesis. Less well known is the fact that the human body is also able to channel the sun, using its energy to produce vitamin D. Known as the "sunshine vitamin," vitamin D isn't really a vitamin. It's a hormone that the body produces when sunlight strikes the skin.[4] Vitamin D helps the digestive system absorb calcium and phosphorous, nutrients that are vital to the maintenance of healthy bones. Recent studies have shown that the positive health impacts of vitamin D extend far beyond healthy bones. Low levels of vitamin D have been linked to high blood pressure, heart failure, statin-related muscle pain, and infection; it has also been tentatively associated with diabetes, osteoporosis, asthma, and memory loss.[5]

THE CIRCADIAN CLOCK

When Marie describes humans as solar powered, she isn't far off. In fact, our bodies run on a twenty-four-hour cycle of waking and sleeping hours, determined by a system known as the "circadian clock." (Technically, the cycle is a little more than twenty-four hours: hence the name, which is Latin for "approximately a day.")

The "solar battery" of the circadian clock is the pineal gland, an endocrine gland in the brain's center. The pineal gland produces the hormone melatonin, which has been linked to reproduction, the immune system, and the cardiovascular system, but is known as the "sleep hormone" because it is the nightly rise in melatonin that makes us sleepy. Melatonin supplements are Steve's remedy of choice to help him with jet lag.

Actually, the pineal gland works more like a reverse solar battery. During the day, special photoreceptive (sun-sensitive) cells in our eyes send signals to the pineal gland, stopping it from producing melatonin. Even electric lights can reduce melatonin production—as can caffeine, which is one of the reasons that coffee makes us feel energized and keeps us awake.[6] At night, when there is less light, melatonin levels begin to rise. This rise tends to begin approximately two hours before we go to sleep, making us tired and leading us to bed.[7]

In addition to managing our daily cycles, the circadian clock is sensitive to seasonal changes in sunlight. We will see how decreases in sunlight during the winter can increase melatonin production and make people feel lethargic or depressed. In spring, as days get longer, melatonin levels decrease. Scientists believe that this drop in melatonin also may be part of what makes animals start mating in spring.[8]

A well-balanced internal clock is important for physical and mental health. Studies have shown that infants sleep better when they are exposed to sunlight in the afternoon, perhaps because it helps with early establishment of the circadian rhythm.[9] When the rhythm gets off kilter, on the other hand, it can have serious consequences. Studies of night workers, for example, have found that their circadian clock is unable to adjust to the misalignment between their sleep schedules and the cycle of the sun, causing everything from depression and hypertension to cancer.[10] Daylight saving time, aging, travel, and seasonal changes also impact our circadian rhythm.

JET LAG

When we travel, we throw our circadian rhythm out of whack. Most travelers are familiar with jet lag, the feeling of exhaustion and disorientation that comes from traveling across time zones, and the malady that contributed to Steve's severe health problems. The technical term for jet lag is "circadian misalignment." What happens is that the melatonin cycle in your body fails to match the time of sunset and sunrise, so you are bombarded with sunlight when you should be feeling tired, or you are wildly awake in the dark, both of which confuse the pineal gland.[11]

The planet spins from west to east, and this is the cycle to which our bodies have become accustomed. This is why traveling west tends to put more strain on our bodies. Typically, it takes twenty-four hours to recover from each one-hour time zone crossed.[12]

If we think back to what happened to Steve, it's clear why his body began to feel the strain of his travel patterns. Steve often traveled from his family's Midwestern home, in the central time zone, to Japan, fourteen hours ahead. When it was 10 A.M. in the United States, it was midnight in Japan. Traveling between the United States and Japan ten times a year would have required Steve to upset his circadian clock by fourteen hours twenty times a year—and Steve traveled much more than that! Over the years, his body became less able to tolerate these disruptions, and it is likely that the constant stress impacted his body's ability to maintain homeostasis and fight off disease. Today, Steve uses melatonin as a supplement to help his body maintain a regular sleep cycle when he travels.

DAYLIGHT SAVING TIME MAY HURT MORE THAN IT HELPS

Daylight saving time is another case of circadian misalignment. The idea behind daylight saving time is to allow for the most number of daylight hours, shifting them from the morning to the evening, when more people are awake and going about their business. There are also assumed benefits in terms of energy savings, preventing traffic accidents due to poor visibility, and even, perhaps, decreasing crime rates. But we all know how disorienting daylight saving time can be. Sudden dark mornings or bright evenings can be confusing to anyone with a regular schedule. Like jet lag, this disorientation is thought to be caused by a disruption to the circadian clock. In this case, our bodies stubbornly remain linked to sunrise and sunset despite society's attempt to shift the day forward or back.

A series of studies examining the period immediately following daylight saving time has found, however, that this seemingly minor circadian shift has different consequences. Scientists determined that there are more car accidents and more workplace injuries, and that workers are less efficient in the week following the shift to daylight saving time. They also found more tentative correlations with heart attacks and suicides.[13]

The benefits of shifting our schedule twice a year are murky, and the practice remains controversial. With this in mind, in 2005, Connecticut state representative Richard Roy proposed keeping daylight saving time year-round. "I was hoping it would cheer people up," he said.[14] Connecticut wasn't ready for annual cheer, however, and Roy was forced to drop the proposal. He said that he hopes to bring it up again in the future.

Daylight saving time is an issue in Mexico as well, but attempts to impose it there ended in failure. In the summer of 1997, President Ernesto Zedillo used his executive powers to bring Mexican clocks into alignment with daylight saving time, setting clocks one hour forward. He was responding to reports that daylight saving time would save money on energy. But the Mexican people were jarred by the shift, and many believed that it was physically and mentally harmful. A nationwide poll conducted by the University of Guadalajara found that 53 percent of the respondents believe that the time change caused "'some type of biological alteration,' including drowsiness, headaches, and more stress."[15]

The time change caused such deep discontentment that some Mexican states rebelled, simply refusing to change their clocks or changing school and work schedules so that the energy-saving measure was made moot. The country's three primary cities, Mexico City, Monterrey, and Guadalajara, protested the change in 1999 and demanded that the order be revoked.

"I just couldn't get used to it," said Ricardo Enciso Aguilar, a lawyer in Guadalajara who worked on the campaign to end daylight saving time. "I began having strange depressions. I felt disoriented and went around half asleep all the time. Mexicans are not accustomed to such drastic change."[16] But, ten years later, daylight saving time remains in place.

RELATIONSHIPS TO THE LIGHT CHANGE
WITH AGE AND ILLNESS

As people get older, their relationships with the sun change. Marie told me, "I think winter and age, darkness and age, they're somehow very closely linked." For Marie, this association is deeply symbolic. When we're young, she observes, there seem to be unlimited possibilities before us. But as we age, the shortening days of winter become a sort of metaphor, or natural manifestation, of a shortening life and fewer possibilities.

Marie found that as she entered her forties, it was increasingly difficult to keep her energy levels high and consistent. The darkness of winter makes her continually aware of this change. "When I don't get this extra boost of energy from the natural light and from the long day, I'm kind of forced to rely on my own battery pack," she says. "And that's when I realize that that battery is not running at the same speed that it used to."

Marie's sensitivity to changes in her body's "battery pack" is accurate. The physical effects of aging, from eyes to brain, impact the pineal gland. They cause older brains to produce less melatonin, and cause the melatonin cycle to shift later into the night. These changes explain why we tend to sleep for less time and less deeply as we get older.[17] They may also explain why in the last three or four years, Marie has started to notice a changing relationship with the sun: she feels a stronger need for it than ever before in her life.

Alzheimer's patients exhibit a unique response to the cycle of the sun. This response is known as "sundowning," and it is characterized by increased arousal in the late afternoon, evening, or night. Thought to be caused by a disturbance in patients' internal clocks, it is associated with degradation of the pineal gland.

Sundowning can range from agitation to complex behaviors. In one case of sundowning, a woman reported that her mother would get anxious many afternoons. After the mother slipped out of the house one day and started trying to feed chickens that weren't there, her daughter realized her mother's agitation was linked to her childhood, when her family had raised hens and fed them every day in the late afternoon. Although the chickens were long gone, the mother's Alzheimer's made her remember the importance of that chore. In another case, a woman left her nursing home, went to a nearby restaurant, and attempted to purchase a bus ticket. After some consideration, this woman's daughter realized that when she was young the mother had left the school where she taught every Friday afternoon and caught a bus home to her parents' house. Many years later, confused by her dementia, she was attempting to relive this tradition.[18]

TOO MUCH OF A GOOD THING

You can have too much of a good thing, and in the case of sunlight the risk of skin cancer is the obvious price that sun lovers pay for their vitamin D. Sunlight can have other deleterious effects, too. It may surprise those who suffer from some degree of winter depression to learn that suicide rates tend to be notably higher in the summer. Studies have found this to be the case in such disparate places as Canada, Hong Kong, Taiwan, Australia, Chile, South Africa, and Greenland; other studies have suggested that this correlation is more developed in higher latitudes, where summer days reach remarkable lengths.

Scientists have proposed several reasons for this pattern. They suggest that while melatonin suppression can make you feel more energetic, it can also cause mild or severe insomnia, leading to exhaustion. They have also found that prolonged sunlight increases serotonin levels in the blood, which can cause violence in men. Finally, cultural behaviors associated with summer, particularly excessive drinking, might impact suicidal behavior.[19]

For Marie, as much as she loves sun, it can sometimes be overstimulating. She can have trouble calming herself and trouble sleeping. She has to channel the energy and use it in order not to be overwhelmed by it.

A Brief History of the Dark and Its Emotional Effects

"Why do you think people migrate south?" a friend once asked me. Answering her own question, she said, "We want to be where it's bright. In winter, when the days are dark and short, you start to feel like you're in a tunnel. And you can't really get out without moving south."

If sunlight is associated with a range of positive physical experiences, darkness is associated in our minds with a list of negative effects. While the winter cold can be oppressive, for many people it is the darkness that wears them down, especially with schedules where the workday is bracketed by night.

My patient Simon feels this way. I talked about Simon in chapter 3, describing how the Jewish holidays play a central role in his difficult relationship with autumn. Regarding winter, he says, "My rabbi used to talk about how every religion has a festival of the lights during December. And this is because

December can be such a depressing month." Holidays may be a dark spot on some people's emotional calendar, but they can also be moments of light during a dark time of the year.

The concept of seasonal mood disorders has existed for a long time. Psychiatrist Leo Sher has found observations about them dating back to the Greek philosopher Posidonious, who wrote almost two thousand years ago that "melancholy occurs in autumn, whereas mania in summer." By the second century, he noted, Greco-Roman physicians treated depression with the application of sunlight toward the eyes. References to seasonal disorders can also be found in the writings of polar explorer Frederick Cook, whose sailors exhibited a loss of sexual desire, fatigue, and a depressed mood. The French neurologist Jean-Étienne-Dominique Esquirol and the German psychiatrist Emil Kraepelin both wrote about seasonally shifting moods in the nineteenth and early twentieth centuries.[20]

"Polar night" is the term used to describe a period of time during winter in the high latitudes when the sun never rises. In Fairbanks, Alaska, the winter solstice is marked by a day when the sun never crosses the horizon. In St. Petersburg, Russia, this period of darkness lasts for a week. In the city of Thule, Greenland, the polar night lasts for four months.

In the late 1800s, the French ethnographer Jean Malaurie spent many years working among the indigenous people of northern Greenland. During his first autumn in Thule, Malaurie reported experiencing headaches and nausea, feelings that he associated with the changing of the seasons. He also wrote of *perlerorneq*, or polar hysteria, a mental disorder that he observed among the indigenous population. *Perlerorneq* generally occurs during the transitional period between autumn and winter. Traditionally, this was an uncomfortable season during which it was too cold to kayak, but the ice bridges that liberate Greenland had not yet frozen solid. It also signified the approach of a particularly dangerous hunting season for men and a season of confinement for women.

Malaurie describes one case of polar hysteria he observed, when a woman suddenly fell into wild and irrational behavior and ran out into the snow. Citing his Eskimo source, he writes that "*perlerorneq* is to be sick of life," adding that it is caused by an excess of introspection brought on by the transition into winter.[21] More recent studies suggest that the indigenous term *perlerorneq* has been misapplied by Western researchers to describe a variety of mental disorders caused by a variety of factors. Still, it remains likely that in some cases *perlerorneq* is a shamanistic, cathartic, or psychotic episode linked to environmental stresses brought on by the approach of the dark season.[22]

During an expedition in the Antarctic, Captain Frederick Cook also observed certain seasonal ailments among his crew. Cook's ship *Belgica* was battered repeatedly by winter storms. Trying for a farthest-south record, the crew ended up closed in by pack ice at sea. There was no way out, no canals of open water. The crew was forced to spend the entire polar night drifting helplessly among huge icebergs.

As time went on, the men began to suffer various health problems. They exhibited spongy gums, puffy eyes and ankles, and pale and oily faces. They complained about headaches, insomnia, indigestion, loss of appetite, and shortness of breath. The condition, which Cook diagnosed as being a type of polar anemia, was a precursor to scurvy. He wisely promoted dietary improvements that mimicked what he had observed the Eskimos eating to stay healthy, including fresh meat.

But Cook also attributed the symptoms to the "prolonged darkness" the crew was experiencing, which he theorized "disturbed the body's equilibrium." His cure for this? He would place a man naked in front of a hot fire for an hour or more. He called it a "baking treatment."[23] This could be the first recorded instance of light therapy being used to cure physical and mental distress brought on by winter.[24]

Today, I would diagnose at least some of Cook's crew with seasonal affective disorder. SAD was named by the doctors Norman Rosenthal and Thomas Wehr in 1984 to describe a syndrome of depression that occurred during the autumn or winter. Symptoms of SAD include feeling depressed and lethargic, with sufferers often sleeping longer than normal. They also tend to crave carbohydrates, which leads to weight gain. Their lack of energy makes them withdraw socially and lose interest in sexual activity. Many of these symptoms are ways that the body normally adapts to cold, but in people with SAD these effects are excessive, disrupting their daily lives. By spring, most of the people who suffer from SAD start to feel more normal again, until the cycle repeats.

Seasonal affective disorder occurs among 4 to 10 percent of the general population, and it strikes women far more frequently than men.[25] SAD is listed in the Diagnostic and Statistical Manual of Mental Disorders (DSM-IV) as "recurrent major depressive episodes with regular seasonal patterns," but it is commonly associated with minor depressive episodes as well.[26] Symptoms include depression, fatigue, loss of interest in sex, increased carbohydrate consumption, and weight gain.[27]

As you might expect, your likelihood of suffering from SAD depends on where you live. In general, people in Florida like winter better than people in New Hampshire: in one study, 48.7 percent of New Hampshire residents "felt worse in the winter months" compared to 17.6 percent of Floridians. And 9.7 percent of the New Hampshire residents passed the official diagnostic criteria for SAD, compared to 1.4 percent of those in Florida. On the other hand, several studies suggest that people who hail from the extreme north (such as Iceland) may be genetically protected from SAD, while the risk of SAD is particularly high among people who are born in southern climes and move north.[28]

LaDonna: I Felt as if Someone Had Stolen the Sun

As a child growing up in southern Illinois, LaDonna Green Bates never hated winter because the cold was accompanied by lots of sunshine. In fact, when she wants to remember something positive from her childhood, she often goes back to a winter day when she was around seven or eight years old, staying home from school because of a snowstorm. "Nothing was moving because we didn't have street cleaners, and everything was just this brilliant white. It seemed like the sunniest day that I had ever seen in my short life. There were no clouds in the sky and I can remember seeing the icicles that were dripping down the house. The sun on them was glistening. It looked like the ground was covered with diamonds. At some time in the afternoon, I lay down on my parents' bed, where a shaft of sunlight was coming in, and I just drank up the sunlight. I felt so good and I drifted off to sleep."[29]

When she moved to St. Louis to attend college, winter seldom bothered her there, either. She took ski vacations on sunny slopes in Colorado and Wyoming. Only after she married Bill Bates and moved to Pittsburgh, Pennsylvania, his hometown, did she begin to feel the effects of the weather. It was 1972, the year she turned thirty.

"I distinctly remember writing to my parents and saying, 'I feel as if someone has stolen the sun,'" she says. "The reason it kind of stands out is that it was the middle of October. I always loved the fall, when the humidity dried out. I loved the changing colors of the leaves. It was kind of energizing to me."

But that year, Pittsburgh seemed to be shrouded in haze, and she felt like the city's low cloud cover was pressing down on her head. "I wanted to load up on carbohydrates in a way that I never ate before. And I was puzzled by that. It was like someone else inhabited my body," she says. Her newfound craving for bread and potatoes led her to gain weight. She didn't know what to do about her reaction to the change of seasons then, or in subsequent years. She simply told herself, "It's gloomy in Pittsburgh, and I need to suck it up and cope with it." This went on for a few years. "I would feel depressed in the winter, and then I would feel wonderful in March or April." Sometimes, she and Bill traveled during the winter or early spring, and this gave her "a burst of sun," which would set her "on a good path" until November or December.

Bill, on the other hand, thrives in Pittsburgh's climate. Raised in the city in the 1940s and 1950s, he became accustomed to constant pollution from the steel mills, and he calls overcast days his "comfort zone." "You can go back and look at pictures from that time, and even on a bright sunny day you could not actually see the sun. And it was not unusual for the men who worked outside the home to bring two clean dress shirts to work in an office and change during the day."

While LaDonna dreads fall in Pittsburgh because she knows the darkness of winter is coming, Bill says fall is his favorite season. He likes "when it's getting dark, when the trees are changing, when it's getting crisp. And my next favorite season is winter. And probably my least favorite season is spring. I don't like all this blossomy, sunny stuff. I finally get used to it by summer."

Bill is the opposite of most people, who on rainy days hope the weather clears up. "I love it when it's raining," he admits. "I feel cheated when it stops and the sun comes out." He walks two to three miles each afternoon in all weather, but he doesn't like the sun "blaring down" on him. "I feel a little more relaxed and good when it's raining. I love walking in the rain. I have nice waterproof rain shoes, a Gore-Tex rain hat, a rain coat. So I love it on days when I can go out and do my midafternoon walk in the rain. It's very cleansing." Though he has lived in other cities, Bill feels entirely at home in Pittsburgh's climate. "I'm used to it. Maybe it's nature versus nurture," he says.

Still, he and LaDonna both faced challenging weather in the winter of 1977. Pittsburgh went through a cold spell so severe that coal barges froze in the river. LaDonna, who was freelancing at the time, conserved heat during the day by confining herself to one room of the house. She ended up becoming clinically depressed and suicidal, and had to be hospitalized for treatment. She says her symptoms were different during this bout of clinical depression than during her typical seasonal winter blues. For example, she didn't want to sleep or eat much during the clinical depression, which was opposite to her usual winter symptoms. Though the clinical depression never recurred ("Thank God—it was horrendous"), her winter blues did continue to resurface each year, distressing her enough to seek treatment.

Her quest for a diagnosis was not easy. "The doctors would humiliate me time and again," she remembers. They dismissed her symptoms as without biological basis. Her research turned up few clues. "There was nothing written. I'd never seen anything about winter blues or about people getting depressed in the winter. So I didn't have any mental hook to hang it on." In the meantime, she became a mother and coped with winter as best she could as she raised her two children.

In 1991, she finally came across a magazine article that described all of her symptoms and provided a name for her condition: seasonal affective disorder. For LaDonna, finding a diagnosis felt tremendously liberating. "Anything is better if it has a name," she says. "Having a name [for a problem] gives you a sense of understanding, even if it doesn't give you a sense of control."

The Science of SAD

What causes seasonal affective disorder? Although we don't know for sure, there is evidence that people with SAD have a problem with their circadian clocks. Ideally, the circadian clock responds to seasonal changes in sunlight, shifting a person's sleep schedule to match natural changes in sunrise and sunset. In people with SAD, however, this shift seems to go overboard as winter approaches. For these people, increased melatonin production brings sleep late at night, causing an evening insomnia. Tiredness and lethargy during the day is a common result.[30]

Problems with melatonin production are compounded in SAD sufferers by a decrease in the mood-controlling neurotransmitter serotonin. Drops in serotonin levels are associated with many kinds of depression. A recent study in Australia, which measured serotonin levels in 101 healthy men over the course of a year, found that serotonin levels are more closely associated with changes in sunlight than with any other environmental factor.[31]

Because SAD is associated with darkness, many SAD sufferers (including Emma) use a light box, a cluster of electric lights that mimic the spectrum of natural light. Light boxes can be used at any time of day, but many people find that morning use seems to simulate dawn and helps to keep the circadian clock on track.[32] LaDonna Bates has devised a number of other ways to expose herself to more natural daylight. When she first learned about SAD, she began walking at lunchtime and sat near windows whenever possible. Her blues lasted only one month that year. When she purchased a light box and used it for about an hour a day, her symptoms all but disappeared. "My children had never seen me happy at Christmas until I got a light box," she says.

Mørketid: The Call to Darkness

For SAD sufferers, the mental disturbances caused by diminishing light can make darkness seem like a terrifying thing. Many people, however, are attracted to the idea that life is meant to be aligned with the cycle of the sun, and feel that night, as well as day, has many things to offer. These are the people who travel to places such as Natural Bridges National Monument, in Utah, or Acadia National Park, in Maine, to seek out the night sky undimmed by light pollution.[33] Some look for experiences of light and darkness that are a little more dramatic. They travel to extreme latitudes, seeking out places where the sun never rises.

In the Arctic, the relationship between time and sunlight is totally redefined. The Greenland Inuit calendar is a striking interpretation of "solar calendars"—each month refers literally to the movement of the sun. The cycle of the year goes from *Qaamaliaq*, January, "month of the moon," to *Ulluujuarsaat*, "the day returns," to autumnal *Tutsarfik*, "we listen," and finally to the month of the winter solstice, *Qaumasigssoq*, "the very luminous one."[34] In the language of the Inuit of Greenland, the word *sila* means both weather and consciousness.[35] In a world where technology has made it possible to live comfortably in a life totally separate from weather and climate, the idea of a place where sun, moon, and storm are totally intertwined with humanity can be appealing.

The city of Tromsø, Norway, is known as the "gateway to the Arctic." At a latitude of nearly 70 degrees north, Tromsø is also known for being home to the northernmost university, cathedral, and eighteen-hole golf course in the world.[36] Countless Arctic expeditions have started here. Although the climate in Tromsø is generally mild, with temperatures ranging from an average of 25 degrees Fahrenheit in the winter to 82 degrees Fahrenheit in the summer, days in this Norwegian city are extreme. During the summer, Tromsø experiences two months of midnight sun, from mid-May to mid-July, when the sun is still visible at midnight. At this time, the city hosts a Midnight Sun Marathon, where tourists and locals can run all day—and all night.

In contrast, from November 21 to January 21, Tromsø experiences polar nights, days when the sun never rises. This two-month period, which is called the *mørketid* and translated alternately as the "dark times" or the "murky times," is not always viewed by locals in the way that outsiders might expect. One reporter who visited Tromsø in December asked his guide about the winter nights. "How do people cope with the polar nights?" he asked. "Don't they become suicidal or insane?"

"Not at all," the guide replied. "Most people here don't believe in seasonal affective disorder—we just prefer to keep busy."[37]

It is perhaps this attitude that draws outsiders to Tromsø. There has recently been a dramatic rise in the number of people visiting the city during the winter months. Between 2004 and 2008, the number of foreign travelers to Tromsø increased by 15.2 percent. The number of winter travelers, however, increased by a remarkable 64.3 percent. Most of these are from

Italy and the United Kingdom, countries known for their mild climates.[38]

While a great deal of this growth comes from business travel, it is possible that employers and individuals alike are drawn to the combination of extreme darkness and active life that makes Tromsø the "Paris of the Arctic." Embracing this apparent oxymoron, the people of Tromsø go out of their way to produce activities and festivals during the *mørketid*, including a rock festival and an international film festival, along with excellent skiing and stunning displays of northern lights. Regarding the appeal that Tromsø holds for southern visitors, a journalist from the *Guardian* puts it best: "I had come to Tromsø out of masochistic curiosity and yet I had warmed to its strange charm. . . . The polar night does not bring out the least desirable elements in human behaviour but some of the best: warmth, friendliness, and a desire to stimulate body and mind."[39]

I have not visited Tromsø but would love to do so. It sounds like a place where night can be as beautiful and full of activity as day!

8

⌒

Wind and Storm:
The Weather of Catastrophe

a wind has blown the rain away and blown

the sky away and all the leaves away,

and the trees stand. I think i too have known

autumn too long

—E. E. CUMMINGS, "a wind has blown the rain away and blown"

WIND, LIKE THE cold, is one of those environmental phenomena that have a tremendous effect on our emotions. It's much easier, however, for people to recognize and quantify the influence that temperature and sunlight have upon them; wind is more subtle but often more powerful in its effects. Storms, on the other hand, are all too obvious and visible in their results. Both wind and storms can have an immediate impact on our emotions and make a long-term mark on our emotional calendars.

Wind Turbulence

Wind is energy. My friend Marie's apartment looks over the Charles River in Boston, and the late afternoon sun slants in during the afternoon. "Some days the river is just flat calm. And then there are days when you look out when it's windy and the water looks dark but is white-capping," she says. "It has nothing to do with the temperature. It has everything to do with the wind stirring it all up, and it feels turbulent and kind of ominous and scary."

Marie is right, of course, about wind and energy. Energy from the sun is transferred to the earth, and as the energy seeks to equalize itself across the surface of the planet, air moves in complicated patterns of circulation. The presence of mountains, valleys, bodies of water, and deserts leads to differences in heating and cooling that result in dynamic and powerful local winds. These include the Santa Ana in southern California, a wind that "shows us how close to the edge we are," as Joan Didion writes. There are the chinooks in the Pacific Northwest and Canada; the foehn near the Alps, a hot, dry wind that is associated with nervousness and anxiety;[1] the mistral in France, which is known as "masterly" for its destructive power; and the sirocco of the Mediterranean, which is a "hot, evil" wind.[2]

Winds have rich mythological energy, too, and the stories about them often involve feelings of turbulence, anxiety, and fear. How could they not? Wind has tremendous power, which can be seen only in the effects it produces, not in and of itself. In Thomas Mann's *Death in Venice*, a classic of Western literature, an aging German writer impetuously travels to Venice, where he becomes infatuated with a young Polish boy. The "sickness" that invades his body and soul is mirrored in the foul winds of the sirocco. Mann writes:

> A revolting sultriness could be felt in the alleys, the air was so heavy that the odors that emanated from the apartments, stores and cookshops, like those of hot oil, clouds of perfume and many more, remained fixed like clouds without dispersing. . . . The longer he walked, the more that disgusting condition took hold over him which is effected by the sea breeze and the sirocco and which is excitement and fatigue at the same time. He began to sweat unpleasantly. The eyes ceased to function, his chest felt tight, he was febrile, his pulse was pounding in his head.[3]

Cholera soon takes hold, the malady filling the air with "a sickly sweet smell reminiscent of distress and wounds and suspicious cleanliness." He feels as if "wind spirits of an evil kind were at work," digging like "ugly seabirds" in his food and contaminating it with putrid disease.[4]

Though wind can be full of evil spirits, it can also appeal to our spiritual sensibility. Traveling to and from Nantucket on the ferry, I always take the opportunity to venture outside on deck. I know that the feeling of wind rushing past my face can be thrilling.

For Marie, the turbulence of the wind can be deeply spiritual. "Sometimes I find it to be cleansing," she says. "Sometimes I'm kind of hoping it will be emotionally cleansing, like blowing through and cleaning out my life." Marie also associates her relationship with the wind to her experience as a sailor. "When it gets really windy and the puffs are really strong, you're less in control. The tiller is harder to manage, and the whole energy of the boat changes. You're getting bounced around. The sail's in, the sail's out, the wind direction's all shifted. But when you have a nice summer day going downwind, you have that sense of possibility, of going in a direction that's infinite."

The Science of Wind

For centuries, wind has been associated with emotional and physiological instability. Yet Western science has been unable to identify a correlation between wind and many wind-related complaints.

Wind can certainly have an effect on our biology. It can alter the body's heat-exchange abilities, increase evaporation, and affect surface circulation of the blood—all elements associated with homeostatic regulation. When wind speed rises above 12 miles per hour, which is not a particularly strong wind, people start to become physically uncomfortable. But scientists have not been able to make an association between people's uneasy feelings about wind and disease. A study conducted in 1992 tracked heart attacks in Austria, trying to link them with incidence of the foehn wind, but they could make no clear correlation.[5] A study published in 2000 tried to confirm the perception by many patients living in Canada that chinook winds triggered their migraine headaches, with 79 percent of them reporting that chinooks brought on their suffering.[6] Again, the researchers found only a small correlation between headaches and winds, and that correlation occurred only when wind speed exceeded 38 miles per hour, which is a gale-force wind. When the migraine sufferers were asked to keep track of the time and date of their headaches, scientists were surprised to find that only 21 percent of those who believed their migraines came at the same time as the wind were correct.[7]

Other studies have shown evidence that winds do, in fact, affect our psychological state. Scientists have documented anxiety, paranoia, and irritability among Californians when the Santa Ana blows during the months of September through March, with the peak danger period in October. In a heavily debated study, one group of Israelis demonstrated increases in nausea, migraines, insomnia, and irritability during the sharav, a hot wind that blows across the Mediterranean and the Middle East in May to mid-June and September to October. Another group exhibited fatigue, depression, hypertension, and apathy.[8]

My patient Gloria is a good example of the way culture influences how we experience winds. An American who studied in Switzerland, she told me about the liberating effect of the foehn. "We were blowing up and down the road back to Lugano, where our school was. And my cousin said, 'You know what the foehn winds do? They either make you mad or sexy.' And I like sex, so they sure as hell worked for that." For Gloria, the foehn winds had sex appeal. But for many Swiss, the foehn brings on anxiety and depression: a sign that tradition, as much as science, determines how we feel about winds.

A Lack of Wind Can Cause Trouble

The autumn of 1952 had been one of England's coldest in more than a century, with inches of early snowfall and, in the southern and western parts of the country especially, frigid winds and temperatures that fell as low as 5 degrees Fahrenheit.[9] The people of London and the surrounding counties had been piling extra coal onto their fires for weeks, trying to keep warm. During the first few days of December, the wind disappeared.

In the still air, the heat from the coal fires stayed put, warming the city and its inhabitants. But without the winds that had kept the air circulating, the cold air high in the atmosphere trapped the warmer air below, and with it the pollutants that were released by the burning coal. Thus began the Great Smog of 1952.

When coal is burned it emits great quantities of such toxic chemicals as carbon dioxide, hydrochloric acid, and sulfur dioxide; it also creates a thick, dark smoke that mixes with cooler air particles and becomes fog. By December 5, 1952, the air in and around London had become an opaque, sooty smog so dense that people could not see their own feet, and so profuse that it crept down chimneys and through doors into people's homes. Visibility became so bad that thousands of cars were abandoned on the street. Performances in theaters and concert halls across the city were canceled, sometimes midshow, because audiences could no longer see the stage. Public transportation came to a virtual standstill.[10]

London was already famous for its pea-soup fogs; its citizens had been burning coal on their fires for centuries and were used to the thick haze that hung over the city as a result. Indeed, fog was a major part of London's cultural identity and had become a key feature of the romanticized, literary London known to the world through Charles Dickens and Sir Arthur Conan Doyle. Consider this passage from Dickens's *Our Mutual Friend*:

> It was a foggy day in London, and the fog was heavy and dark. Animate London, with smarting eyes and irritated lungs, was blinking, wheezing, and choking; inanimate London was a sooty spectre, divided in purpose between being visible and invisible, and so being wholly neither. . . . Even in the surrounding country it was a

foggy day, but there the fog was grey, whereas in London it was, at about the boundary line, dark yellow, and a little within it brown, and then browner, and then browner, until at the heart of the City it was rusty-black. From any point of the high ridge of land northward, it might have been discerned that the loftiest buildings made an occasional struggle to get their heads above the foggy sea, and especially that the great dome of Saint Paul's seemed to die hard; but this was not perceivable in the streets at their feet, where the whole metropolis was a heap of vapour charged with muffled sound of wheels, and enfolding a gigantic catarrh.[11]

So Londoners were accustomed to dark, smoggy days, just as they were accustomed to irritation in their lungs and soot seeping into their clothing. It was, therefore, not immediately obvious that this fog was different. But it was different; in fact, it was lethal. By December 9, 1952, nearly five thousand tons of toxic pollution had poured into the air and stayed there.[12] Those with respiratory problems, and the very old and young, were affected first and worst; hundreds died each day from choking or asphyxiating, or from heart attacks due to their inability to breathe the air. But as the days went on and the smog did not dissipate, healthy people began to sicken and die as well. Pneumonia, bronchitis, and asthma attacks became rampant.

Jenny Hamilton was an ambulance coordinator in London during the Great Smog and shared her memories of the experience with the *Mirror*.

The calls started coming in like crazy. . . . It was all the same story: "My wife . . . my husband . . . my children are coughing and can't breathe." They were dying from the fumes. We kept sending ambulances out, but the drivers were telling us they couldn't find their way. People had to carry lamps in front of them so they could get through. We tried to send the medics to where they were most needed, but we simply couldn't cope with demand. The numbers of dead grew and grew. I remember clutching the pink slips which drivers had to fill in after making a call. The same message came back time and time again: "Dead On Arrival."[13]

Jenny Hamilton was in a position to realize just how serious the situation was; most other Londoners were not. It was some days before the city's morticians had run out of coffins, and the florists had run out of flowers because of overwhelming demand for funerals.[14]

At last, on December 9, 1952, a strong westerly wind began to blow, and within a day the deadly fog had dissipated. By the end of those five days, four thousand smog-related deaths had been recorded. In the following months, eight thousand more people died in London and the surrounding area due to illnesses or complications caused by the smog.[15]

When it became apparent that the Great Smog was a direct result of the pollution caused by open coal fires, the government formed the British Committee on Air Pollution, which eventually passed the City of London (Various Powers) Act of 1954 and the Clean Air Acts of 1956 and 1968, the first antipollution legislation in history.[16] Several more poisonous fogs descended on London in following years, including one in 1962 that killed 750 people. But it was the unique weather conditions immediately before and during the Great Smog of 1952 that made it so uniquely deadly. And while the antipollution laws have largely solved the problem in England, similar smogs have formed over such major cities as Los Angeles, Beijing, and Mexico City, and it may be only a matter of time before a wind-and-weather combination brings death to thousands again.

Health and Storms

Too much wind, of course, can also be a major problem for people and cause damage to the places where they live. Human health is highly sensitive to stormy weather. The amount of water in the air—in the form of fog, mist, clouds, rain, snow, sleet, and hail—can negatively affect our physical well-being. Researchers at the Children's Hospital in Boston, for example, found that humidity and temperature were to blame for one in three headaches among study participants, and a further 13 percent were caused by barometric pressure.[17] We saw earlier how humidity can prevent our body's natural cooling system from working fully. Humidity is also blamed for "increased ear wax, sickle-cell anemia, insomnia, gout, respiratory viruses, and rheumatoid arthritis."[18]

Yes, the human body is sensitive to weather. But how sensitive is it? I always thought that the ability of the body to predict weather was pseudoscience. Claims that wounds could give storm warnings, that arthritic joints predicted rain, or that highly attuned olfactory systems could "smell" approaching weather seemed to fall away in the face of scientific fact.

But several studies have proven that it is indeed possible to sense an approaching storm. In one University of Pennsylvania study, volunteers with arthritis were sent to isolated hospital rooms. Then, scientists manipulated the atmospheric pressure and humidity of the rooms, mimicking the conditions prior to a storm. As pressure fell and humidity increased, patients complained that their joints were starting to ache. When they were examined by physicians at the end of the study, it turned out that their joints were actually inflamed.[19]

In another study, scientists at the Smell and Taste Treatment and Research Foundation in Chicago found that, for some people, a rapid pressure change can improve the sense of smell. When people who have lost their ability to smell dive into a pool or fly in an airplane, they sometimes experience an "olfactory window," a brief period of time during which they can smell again. Perhaps this is what happens during storms, with changes in barometric pressure heightening some people's sense of smell. This increase in smell sensitivity may be enough to give particularly aware individuals the ability to "smell" the approach of a storm.[20]

Kids and Weather Fear

Weather is an uncontrollable force with incredible destructive power. For children in particular, weather can be a source of anxiety that has the potential to become a debilitating phobia.

Dr. Susan Mortweet VanScoyoc, a board-certified specialist in behavioral psychology, has worked with children suffering from various types of anxieties. She spoke with us about some of the weather anxieties that she observed in her practice, which was located in the Midwest, where the predominant threat is of thunderstorms and tornados. Growing up, she said, she had a cousin whose father was anxious about weather. "Her dad would call us even when we were away at college if there were any kind of weather reports for our area to make sure we knew how to stay safe. My cousin, who now has children of her own, displays similar weather anxieties, even if it's not on a conscious level. Even at this level it interferes with her life."[21] For most people, weather anxiety remains at this subthreshold level. In some people, however, this anxiety can reach levels so debilitating that it becomes a diagnosable anxiety disorder.

VanScoyoc believes that weather anxieties in children tend to come from parents who exhibit anxieties of their own relating to weather. "There's rarely an anxious child that doesn't have anxious parents," she explained. The parents may not have diagnosable anxieties, but "certainly their behaviors have told their children how to respond to weather." It is a fine line, in her experience, between helping a child and reinforcing his or her anxiety. "You want to protect them when it's storming and, of course, letting them climb in bed with you and snuggling them up in your arms feels right. Instinctively you want to let them know they're safe and protected. Or you decide not to send your child to soccer practice because it is threatening to rain. Before you realize it, you may have a child that's overwhelmed by the slightest hint of inclement weather, panicking in the classroom because he has to go outside when it's cloudy, but just can't."

Using the American Psychiatric Association's criteria for a specific phobia, VanScoyoc and her colleague Dr. Edward Christophersen have published examples of weather-specific phobias in children. These include "overwhelming feeling of dread present when a few clouds are in the sky," "excessive fear of an impending storm" despite rational reassurance, and avoidance of outdoor activities such as recess or ball practice.

Julia: Thunder Panic

Although children are particularly sensitive to weather, storm phobias are not unique to kids. Julia is a twenty-three-year-old woman from Long Island who suffers from what she describes as a "very, very sharp startle response." Ever since she was a child, she has been extremely sensitive to loud noises but, she says, storms are the worst because they're so drawn out.

Julia's response begins with anticipatory anxiety. Because storms tend to occur in the summer in New York, hot and humid weather makes her feel anxious day and night. If she hears about an impending storm on the weather report, she will start getting nervous. The first rumbles of thunder will trigger a panic attack. "My stomach drops, my heart rate goes up. My breathing will be very labored," she says. Her senses go into overdrive, and, she says, "I can't keep [my eyes] closed. I'm so tense that there's an instinct to notice everything around me."

The duration of her thunderstorm-related panics depends on the length of the storms, but it always takes Julia a few hours to feel normal again. "Afterward, I'm very, very tense and stressed. My whole body seizes up, and it takes me a long time to loosen up again."

Not surprisingly, Julia's least favorite season is summer, when thunderstorms occur most frequently. Hot and humid weather generally upsets her. While growing up and attending school, she says, "I avoided weather reports. And if I did hear one, I would have anticipatory anxiety." Even now, starting in May each year, she tends to be more tense and have trouble sleeping. She stays indoors a lot and looks forward to the onset of autumn, when the worst of her weather triggers are over for the year. "About September or around the time school starts, my panic lessens even though that doesn't always mean that the storms are gone." In the dead of January, unless there is a freak thunderstorm, "for the most part, I'm much calmer."

Julia is quick to point out that although she has been sensitive to sound since childhood, she has never been able to find an explanation for why she experiences this intense weather anxiety. What she does know is that it has a huge impact on her daily life. It makes it difficult for her to go out in public. She has a hard time finding a job because employers worry that her phobia will make her a liability. And she was forced to drop out of college because her anxiety made it impossible for her to study.

Julia has never met anyone with the same weather anxiety that she has. "There's definitely a stigma about it," she explains. "It's embarrassing, and most people don't know how to relate to it. They're very insensitive. They make jokes, or when they do try to comfort me, it's really patronizing."

For people like Julia, and for children like Susan Van-Scoyoc's patients, there are ways of treating weather anxiety. Over the years, Julia has developed a number of "tricks" that she uses to help calm herself during any thunderstorm she has the misfortune to encounter. "I use music headsets, and the headset you wear during target shooting to mute the sound of the guns," she says. She has taken antianxiety medication, but it usually puts her to sleep. She describes other "very small measures that make me feel a little bit more in control." These include drawing the curtains, having a blanket over her head if it's really bad, keeping a flashlight near in case the lights go out, and wearing earplugs. But, she points out, these measures don't get to the root of the problem. Her tricks allow her to avoid paying attention to the storm, but "that's paradoxically not such a good thing, because it means I'm not actually dealing with the storm, which delays my recovery."

VanScoyoc agrees, saying that while such techniques can help keep a person calm, they will not resolve full-fledged anxiety. Julia is working to control her anxiety through cognitive behavioral therapy; by the time she is done with therapy, she hopes she won't need to use her tricks anymore.

More Extreme Reactions to Extreme Weather

So far, we have been discussing wind and storms as mild weather events that might make our knees ache or temporarily drown our flower beds. But as we have been reminded several times in the last few years, weather events have the potential to be hugely destructive and traumatic. Hurricanes, tornados, landslides, and floods can have a huge impact on individuals and on communities.

We often think of these extreme storms and their consequences in terms of the environmental damage that they cause: downed trees, flooded streets, wrecked houses, and displaced or dead people. It is less common for us to consider the psychological impact of these storms on the survivors who have to live through their aftermath, often in a physically damaged location and mourning the loss of loved ones.

In the wake of Hurricane Katrina, many survivors exhibited signs of acute stress disorder, or ASD. ASD is a short-term psychological disorder that can be triggered by any kind of traumatic event, from the death of a loved one to a destructive storm. Its symptoms tend to have two phases. In the first phase, sufferers exhibit strong emotional responses, including fright, disbelief, denial, grief, or relief. In the next few weeks, they begin to show second-stage behaviors, including regression, aggression, anxiety, fear, apathy, sadness, and depression, as well as psychosomatic symptoms, such as stomachaches.[22] A study showed that in the case of Hurricane Katrina these symptoms were made worse among children because support systems collapsed. Schools were closed, psychologists were not always available, and family members were unable to provide support because of their own emotional distress.[23]

ASD is a disorder that can last for several weeks or even months but it eventually fades. If symptoms continue, however, the patient may be suffering from post-traumatic stress disorder (PTSD). We usually think of PTSD as something confined to warfare and sexual abuse but, in fact, any traumatic event can cause PTSD. People suffering from PTSD usually exhibit three types of symptoms: "reexperiencing symptoms," "avoidance symptoms," and "hyperarousal symptoms."[24] It is important to recognize that both ASD and PTSD are medically diagnosable mental disorders and can be far more debilitating than the periods of mourning and loss that anyone might experience after a traumatic event.

PTSD sufferers often experience something known as "intrusive memories" or "intrusive thoughts." These thoughts or memories are anxiety inducing, recurring, and uncontrollable. They enter the mind unbidden and cannot be ignored. If you find yourself revisiting an embarrassing event while you're trying to fall asleep at night, you are experiencing a mild version of an intrusive memory. With PTSD this effect is magnified.

The most extreme version of an intrusive memory is known as a "dissociative flashback." When someone is having a flashback, he or she relives the memory of a traumatic event as though it were occurring in the present. Flashbacks tend to be relatively brief and tend to activate the senses, so that a person who has survived a traumatic storm, when experiencing a flashback, actually hears the thunder, smells the rain, and feels the water on his skin. They are usually brought on by a trigger, something that reminds the person of the original event. In the case of a storm, for example, a loud sound might trigger a flashback because it brings back the memory of thunder.[25]

In 2002, a group of scientists examined the quality of flashbacks in PTSD sufferers. They were surprised to find that flashback memories tend to be of the moments preceding the high point of the trauma, rather than the trauma itself. In the case of a stabbing survivor, for example, the flashback might be of the sidewalk, a grassy patch, a brick wall—everything she saw before she was stabbed.

The scientists proposed that perhaps flashback memories serve a protective function. In most people, the mind has the ability to respond rapidly to perceived threats, something that is popularly known as the "fight or flight" response. This is what causes you to jump when you see a snake in the road, long before you realize that it's actually a stick. For people with PTSD, the scientists argued, the mind misinterprets the moments before the event as a warning signal. They subconsciously believe that the image of a brick wall means an attacker is approaching, or that the sound of thunder means the house is about to flood. A flashback is a panic response to this warning signal.[26]

As we will see in part 3, the development of our emotional calendars is closely associated with the way our memories function. Intrusive memories are often triggered by seasonal variables, such as the smell of spring or the touch of snow, and traumatic weather experiences can become hotspots on our emotional calendar. In the next chapter, we will look more closely at memory science to better understand the many layers of our emotional calendars.

The Future of Weather Anxiety

The psychological impact of traumatic weather events can be immense, and it is an unfortunate truth that the risk of these destabilizing events is increasing rapidly. A 2007 report by the Intergovernmental Panel on Climate Change predicts that by the mid-twenty-first century climate change will have led to an increase in the intensity and frequency of extreme weather events such as heat waves and droughts, heavy precipitation, and tropical cyclones around the world.[27]

As the occurrences of these traumatic events increase, it is likely that there will be a subsequent rise in associated anxiety and post-traumatic disorders. While Julia's therapy is helping her cope with her storm anxiety, it is likely that an increase in the frequency of storms and in the length of the storm season will make daily life more difficult for others like her. Researchers in Australia have already observed how an increase in brush fires is causing anticipatory anxiety among farmers there. In addition to preparing communities for the physical damage caused by these events, it is important that we establish effective support systems now that will help people cope with both anticipatory anxiety and the psychological impacts of surviving a traumatic weather event.[28]

As devastating as storms can be to our physical surroundings and to our personal homeostasis, they are also necessary. Torrential rains refill our reservoirs, they keep our fields and riverbanks fertile, and they cleanse rivers and other water bodies that would become stale and polluted otherwise. Lightning causes wildfires that are vital to purging overpopulated and dead plants and stimulating new growth. The world needs storms to stay balanced and functioning at its best.

People need storms, too. Storms shake us out of ourselves a bit; they make us look around at the world and think about things in new and different ways. As Marie pointed out, big storms inspire neighbors to lend a helping hand. They remind us that we are all in this together. Storms also clear the air— physically and metaphorically. In his weekly monologue "The News from Lake Wobegon" on the long-running radio show *A Prairie Home Companion*, Garrison Keillor frequently talks about the weather and the different ways that people respond to it. He often refers to the resentment that builds up when the weather is nice for too long; people, Keillor suggests, need the challenge of bad weather to keep their personal demons at bay.

"There is a lot of bitterness in summer. I don't know why," Keillor told his listeners one Saturday night in July.

> This unhappiness. People wondering why summer isn't more fun when we've been looking forward to it all these months. I say, just wait for a storm to come along. A beautiful summer storm in the Midwest. The sky turns a purplish black, and the clouds come rolling in, a great turmoil in the sky. The radio tells you to seek shelter, but everybody goes out on the lawn to watch it come in. Flashes in the distance and then flashes not so far away, like artillery in the sky, thunder and lightning. And buckets of rain. You need this storm regularly. And it clears everything away. The air is full of ozone. All of your edginess, and dissatisfaction, it's all gone with the storm.[29]

Perhaps even really bad storms, as damaging and sometimes traumatic as they are, are needed to keep our emotional calendars in balance. The stress and anxiety that come with *anticipating* disaster can cause genuine distress of a kind that only the storm itself can ease. This is particularly true in regions that frequently experience hurricanes and tropical storms. In 2006, journalist Graham Brink of the *St. Petersburg Times* wrote about the odd sense of anticlimax that many people experience when they've prepared for a hurricane that then doesn't come. Brink wrote:

No right-minded person wants a hurricane to strike. But the unrealized expectations can leave people perturbed, instead of happy that they got lucky again.

"We tend to think of it as wasted effort and that the preparation was a waste of time," said Charles Figley, director of the Traumatology Institute at Florida State University. "It gets worse with every year that nothing happens."

There is an unmeasured psychological toll paid every time hurricanes threaten, even if the storms miss us again and again. Knowledge may give us power, but it also can make us anxious, aware and afraid of what might happen as that "cone of uncertainty" envelops our lives, season after season.[30]

Whether ruinous or revitalizing, storms are a part of life and an important element of our emotional calendars. It can be helpful to think of them this way and to take note of storms and how you feel about them each time they occur. Your own response may surprise you!

PART III

Emotional Hotspots:
It's That Time of
Year Again

And you would accept the seasons of your heart just as you

have always accepted that seasons pass over your fields

and you would watch with serenity through the winters of

your grief.

—KAHLIL GIBRAN, *The Prophet*

 Emotional hotspots come in many forms. As we saw with Emma, they are tied to the times of year when we are at our most vulnerable and volatile, when we have memories of past experiences that condition us to expect turmoil in our lives. They are the spots on our calendars when we feel least ourselves, and any number of things can make us feel this way.

The physical and environmental factors we talked about in part 2 recur at specific times of year, but they overlap and influence one another, so that the weather is never quite identical on a given date from year to year. While certain types of weather will predictably affect us every time they occur, the extent to which we feel those effects changes. A person like Jenny, say, who is uncomfortable in the heat and dreads summer because of it, will find that both the season and her reactions to it shift in response to changing circumstances. She'll feel enormous relief in a summer when the temperatures rarely get above the midseventies, as sometimes happens where she lives, and her mood will improve drastically as a result. "If every summer was perfect I probably wouldn't have this feeling, because there are certainly many summer days that are very pleasant," she says.

In much the same way, emotional hotspots await us on the calendar in the same places each year, but they can seem different because of extenuating circumstances. So although Emma struggles with her winter depression each year, changes in her mood and general lifestyle can make the struggle better or worse from one winter to the next. Her first winter at college was particularly bad: she had chosen a school in the city, and the dirty snow, gray concrete, and relentless city noise and crowds made coming back from Christmas break nearly unbearable. "I didn't feel very safe," she recalls. "No one was really nice to me there. And the school was just like a dirt pit with all these sirens around because it was near so many hospitals."

The following year, Emma transferred to a school in a much smaller, more suburban town. She was amazed at the change in herself. "I transferred for the spring semester, in the middle of the year, and started in February, and I didn't really have to use my light box as much. You know, I just kind of forgot that

I had it. I was so happy being at this new place. It was bizarre—it was the first time in years that I didn't really have to use my light box."

Bringing about a change in circumstances—whether by moving, making smaller lifestyle changes, or even just adjusting your perspective about the problem—can be an immensely effective way of managing the effects of emotional hotspots, and we'll talk about that at greater length in the final part of the book.

Everyone's emotional calendar is unique, built of genetic disposition and individual experience, and heavily influenced by an extraordinary array of incidents both random and predictable. People's calendars tend to overlap one another's to some extent, based on shared experiences and similar points of view. On the other hand, I have been surprised time and again by cases of close friends, parents and children, and even husbands and wives whose lives and experiences coincide, but who have entirely different physical and emotional responses. This is particularly true of cultural hotspots, such as Christmas or the anniversary of the 9/11 attacks. These are deeply emotional times for many, many people—but most people experience them differently, as we've seen already and as we'll explore further in the coming pages. A profoundly upsetting hotspot to one person might be an especially happy one for somebody else.

There is no telling what episode in your life might become an emotional hotspot later on. Our brains have a complex strategy of recording and retrieving memories, and everything we see, smell, hear, touch, and taste is liable to become a memory that will return every time we experience a similar sensation. When that sensory experience has a strong emotional association attached to it, often a hotspot is born. These memories can affect us differently each time we recall them—sometimes without our even realizing it. There are even times when we are affected by a memory long after we think the experience is well behind us. Emma genuinely believed she was "over" her traumatic breakup and her abusive boyfriend, and that her winter depression really was simply the result of her academic stress and SAD joining forces against her. Yet even now, she sometimes tears up during sessions when we talk about it. Hotspots can be insidious and pervasive, even when we think they're under control.

Just as you cannot predict what events might become hotspots in your future, I cannot tell you what hotspots may already be lurking on your personal emotional calendar. It is up to you to examine your emotions and behavior throughout the year and begin to recognize the patterns that form your own emotional calendar. In the next few chapters, I will illustrate some of the most common and significant hotspots, both positive and negative, that I've seen patients and acquaintances cope with throughout the year, as well as the different strategies they have used to rise above them. I hope you will recognize yourself in some of these stories and gain some insight into what you yourself might be feeling as you proceed through your year.

9

Emotional Memory

One day in winter, on my return home, my mother,
seeing that I was cold, offered me some tea, a thing I
did not ordinarily take. I declined at first, and then, for
no particular reason, changed my mind. She sent for
one of those squat, plump little cakes called "petites
madeleines," which look as though they had been
moulded in the fluted valve of a scallop shell. And soon,
mechanically, dispirited after a dreary day with the
prospect of a depressing morrow, I raised to my lips a
spoonful of the tea in which I had soaked a morsel of
the cake. No sooner had the warm liquid mixed with the
crumbs touched my palate than a shudder ran through
me and I stopped. . . . An exquisite pleasure had
invaded my senses, something isolated, detached, with
no suggestion of its origin. And at once the vicissitudes
of life had become indifferent to me, its disasters
innocuous, its brevity illusory—this new sensation
having had on me the effect which love has of filling me
with a precious essence; or rather this essence was not
in me it was *me.*

—MARCEL PROUST, *Remembrance of Things Past*

OUR EMOTIONAL CALENDAR in the present is irreversibly tied to our past. Look at the ways that so many of the people in this book talk about their emotional hotspots. My patient Emma's winter depression is linked to the memory of breaking up with her boyfriend and to her subsequent severe depression and hospitalization. My friend Marie speaks about fall in terms of school shopping with her mother, although she hasn't been in school for years. Brian's feelings about the winter holidays are forever tied to his struggles with alcoholism.

The same is true with me. My late-August malaise is associated with my expectations for fall and my memories of summer, feelings that reflect years of seasonal anxiety around the summer-to-fall transition, as well as my urge to get the jump on the turn of the season rather than more passively endure the bitter end.

Yet most of us have only a vague understanding of the role that memory plays in our lives. It's easy to think of memories as chapters in a book or photographs in an album. To remember an event, we simply find it in the table of contents, flip to the correct page, and *voilà!* a perfect record of that memory.

But if we take just a moment to think about how we actually remember things, it will be obvious that it's not so simple. Our memories are rarely complete, accurate representations of the past. They have no table of contents, and they can come to us unbidden, unwanted, and even unnoticed. And there are always emotions attached.

Gloria: A Lifetime of Difficult Winter Memories

To understand the way that memory science applies to our emotional calendar, I'd like to take an in-depth look at the story of one of my patients, Gloria. I've already spoken about Gloria in previous chapters because of the complex associations she builds between physical and emotional experiences. Here, I'm going to add some memory concepts that will help explain the web binding these elements together.

Gloria, now sixty, has lived in a one-bedroom condo that overlooks the cityscape of Cambridge for four years, ever since the sudden death of her husband of thirty-two years. Until his death, Gloria and her husband had lived in rural Massachusetts, where they had built and run a horse farm. Gloria spent most of her adult life living in the farmhouse she and her husband had renovated. She loved training and riding the horses, and even prepared for the Olympics as a dressage competitor. Yet within a year of her husband's death, Gloria sold the horse farm and moved to the city.

As much as Gloria loved her husband and enjoyed her equestrian life, she had a difficult time coping with that lifestyle over such a long period of time. She is bipolar, a condition she has suffered from most acutely during the fall and winter throughout her life. She has dark memories of spending time in psychiatric wards during the winter months, and the emotional effects of these experiences continue to influence her mind-set and behavior to this day; she associates fall and winter weather with traumatic episodes of her illness. Thunderstorms remind her of being handcuffed, which she's experienced during bipolar episodes. Hurricanes and especially blizzards make her think of being in a straitjacket. When she experiences days on end without sunshine, or when she dwells on the short, dark days of winter, she feels that she is once again strapped into four-point restraints. The isolated life on the farm, combined with the long, cold, snowy rural winters, frequently made her feel deeply melancholy and desperately lonely.

Gloria's husband had been an extremely controlling man,

and she often found it hard to cope with his demands when she was feeling depressed or anxious. "He was sympathetic to everything I did, except he didn't understand my bipolar disorder," she explains. "Which made things inconvenient." Rather than try to reason with him, or find a way to comply on her own terms, she would simply retreat. So in the winter months, when she was at her worst emotionally, she felt even more isolated because she could not turn to her husband for support and comfort.

Gloria's seasonal troubles begin around Labor Day, because, she says, she starts to think of what lies ahead. On the coast of Massachusetts, where Gloria grew up, late August is marked by the start of hurricane season, a sign that winter is on its way. From that point on through the first day of spring, Gloria faces continual feelings of depression, loneliness, emotional distress, and physical discomfort.

Despite her deep emotional associations with winter, Gloria describes her aversion to the season as a physical problem. Her body is sensitive to cold, and she's always felt that she can't get warm enough in the winter. This was particularly a problem living out in the drafty old farmhouse, especially since her husband wouldn't let her turn the heat up as high as she would have liked. (Now that she's living on her own, she keeps the heat at 80 degrees.) She finds it stressful to get dressed in cold weather. A former model, Gloria likes to look her best, and she finds that impossible when she is hampered by layers of bulky clothing. "I don't like the accoutrements, all the clothes that I have to wear. Just getting them out of storage depresses me," she says. On top of everything else, she says, "I have to go to the bathroom like crazy in the winter." (In fact, animal studies suggest that exposure to cold can lead to bladder muscle overactivity. And a 2005 study by urologists found that cold does seem to increase the urgent need to urinate.[1] As Gloria puts it, "It's just annoying as hell.")

Snow frightens Gloria and makes her feel anxious. "When it snowed [on the farm] it felt like I was trapped. I'd get very depressed. I had lots of friends and my dogs and lots of people working on my farm. But they didn't make any difference. I had old glass windows around the deck. And I'd look out these doors, and the drifts would keep coming and coming."

The combination of recurring physical discomfort and negative emotional associations makes winter very difficult for Gloria. Because the physical aspects seem like a more immediate problem and are easier to control, they are what she focuses on. But it's her memories that cause her debilitating misery.

The Science of Memories

Memory scientists say that our memories are separated into two different categories: non-declarative and declarative.

Non-declarative memory is the memory of things that we don't remember happening: we don't even know we know them. These include basic skills, such as your ability to ride a bike or to play chess. In studies, for example, scientists will give individuals lists of words, containing, say, the word "orange." Later, the subjects are asked to answer questions. Although the study subjects don't remember most of the words on the list, they are highly likely to respond with "orange" when asked to "name a fruit" or "name a word that starts with 'O.'"[2]

How does non-declarative memory impact your emotional calendar? Just because we don't know that we are accessing our non-declarative memory doesn't mean that it's not a part of our daily lives. Daniel Schacter, a specialist on what he refers to as "implicit memory," tells the story of an engineer who had left one company to join a competitor. His original employers sued him, arguing that his implicit memory was accessing engineering secrets and using them to develop technology for their competitor. His memory was stealing company information and he didn't even know it![3] How many decisions in our lives are influenced by knowledge we don't even know we have?[4]

Declarative memories, in contrast, are memories we can talk about. There is a great debate about how to categorize these memories. Many scientists believe that there are several different kinds of declarative memories, which use different neurological mechanisms and should be thought of as distinct processes. Others argue that all declarative memories fall on a spectrum.

On one end of the spectrum are semantic memories—memories of facts and figures. If you know your name, that's a semantic memory. If you know what year John F. Kennedy died, that's a semantic memory. So is the name of the current president of the United States, your knowledge of the force of gravity, and the millions of other bits of data stored in your brain.

On the other end of the spectrum are episodic memories. Does somebody's name remind you of a beloved relative? Do you remember how you felt the day JFK died? How about the day the president was elected? Now you are accessing your episodic memory. Episodic memories are memories of things that have happened to us. They combine sensory data, emotional resonances, and factual information. Endel Tulving, one of the pioneers of the theory of episodic memory, described it as "a true, even if as yet generally unappreciated, marvel of nature."[5] According to Tulving, humans are unique among animals because they have the ability to create episodic memories. And it is episodic memory that allows us to "travel back in time" by reliving our pasts.[6]

Episodic memories can also cause us to relive our pasts in unwelcome ways. When we have a recurring response at a certain time of year—whether a type of weather, a physical ailment, or an emotional difficulty is at the root of the issue—that response is always influenced by the memory of our emotions during similar past events. Gloria, for example, is wary of snowstorms and associates snow with the feelings of isolation and imprisonment she experienced living in the country. She feels depressed and anxious throughout the winter, even though she now lives in a condo in the city. The streets are cleared and the sidewalks are shoveled, and she can get out and about easily, yet she still feels the old sense of dread when the flakes start to fall.

"If my friends have tickets for something and the weather turns out stormy that day, I really work toward canceling out. They call me unreliable," she says. "I just panic."

ENCODING YOUR MEMORIES

Imagine you're at a wedding reception. The bride and groom have hired a professional filmmaker, who is recording snippets of conversation. In a corner, a couple of kids are playing with their mother's digital camera. A catering service has printed out a menu, a small band is playing the second set, and guests are writing notes in a memory book in the lobby. At the end of the party, everyone goes home. The mother dumps all the pictures onto her desktop. The caterer files her menu in a folder. The memory book is placed in the closet. The filmmaker edits the snippets into a video. And there all that stored material sits until somebody wants to remember a certain moment.

This is like the memory process. Each of our senses—touch, taste, sight, smell, and sound—records snippets of conversation, snapshots of events, flavors of a meal. These bits of sensory input are scattered across our brain in compartments that specialize in certain types of information. Sound goes to one part of the brain, taste to another, and so on. Scent is unique because the olfactory nerve, where memories of scent are stored, is a weblike organ that spreads throughout the brain.

Because of the way that our sensory input is stored in different parts of our brain, our memories might be thought of as constellations of data stored throughout our minds. When we remember something, we activate a network that draws all of these pieces back together and creates a story. Some of the pieces are old and dusty. Other pieces are lost or broken beyond repair. So our brain fills in the gaps and uses whatever information it has to tell the story of a past event. This reconstruction is unique each time it occurs. Our brains come up with different pieces of information depending on our moods, just as it fills in gaps with different filler information, such as related emotions from similar memories.

Thus Gloria, in speaking about her late husband, recalls him differently depending on the emotions that a specific memory triggers. When she thinks of her marriage in general terms, she says, "He was a wonderful man in trying to please me." The foxhunt pattern on the set of fine china in her home reminds her of her husband, because, she says mischievously, "We were always chasing each other around and around." Yet when asked about him in the context of her memories of winter, her tone changes entirely. "My husband and I didn't get along," she says. And of feeling imprisoned in her house during snowstorms, she adds, "Well, I was in an unhappy marriage. So there was no escape."

RETRIEVING YOUR MEMORIES

How does one recall a memory? Memory retrieval, of course, is a little more complicated than looking in a table of contents, but there are useful comparisons. When we try to remember something, we look for the piece of information that will unlock that knowledge—the index entry that will lead us to the correct page. Sometimes that index entry is factual. Sometimes it is sensory, a smell or a feeling. And sometimes it is emotional.

Gloria has learned to tap into the power of memory to help herself survive the winter months. When she was younger, winter holidays to the Caribbean were an oasis of peace. Many of her happiest memories are of the bright, hot, colorful days she's spent there. She now tries to bring back specific memories of the Caribbean when she is feeling particularly depressed in winter. To help trigger these memories and re-create her joyful mood, she listens to reggae music, sits among the bright orange and yellow throw pillows on her couch, and looks at pictures from her vacations. "When I want to dream about being warm and sunny, I listen to reggae," she says.

A trigger is a bit of information that activates the full recollection of a memory. Sometimes a trigger can come upon you unannounced. Understanding this process is key to understanding the emotional calendar, because it is the association between a trigger and a memory that gives emotional resonance to so many parts of the year.

Marcel Proust's "petites madeleines" story is a famous example of this kind of accidental memory retrieval. Proust dips a small cake into his tea and is suddenly transported into a state of rapture. As it turns out, the flavor of the cake reminds him of his youth, an apparently happy time when he would eat madeleines dipped in tea. But at the moment, Proust has no idea why he is feeling so overjoyed. The flavor triggered an emotional response that was part of a sensory memory network.

This experience is common for many people. I once had a patient who always felt sad on the Fourth of July. It was only after some lengthy discussion that he came to realize it was because he associated all the flag images with a patriotic friend who had died. He had never thought of his friend in terms of his

patriotism while he'd been alive. It was only implicitly that the
memory caused my patient to associate Independence Day with
his friend. This revelation explained why he was feeling off, and
the knowledge was a comfort to him in facing the problem. He
took time to actively mourn his friend, and then he was able to
go out and enjoy the parade.

How Gloria Manages Her Memories

For many years, Gloria used what Harvard psychologist George
Vaillant calls "neurotic defenses"[7] to cope with the close associations that she drew between her unhappy marriage, her
bipolar disorder, and her aversion to winter. She would withdraw
into herself, avoiding her husband's guests when they came to
visit. She'd pretend nothing was wrong, that she was busy with
other things. She hated having to show her husband's guests
around the farm when it was cold and snowy. "I'd do anything to
avoid going out and getting cold. I was always looking for ways
to escape," she says.

Gloria and I meet weekly for psychotherapy and discussion
of her psychopharmacologic treatment. Although she used to be
isolated and full of quirky, ineffective responses to her seasonal
mood fluctuations, she is now much calmer and more secure
that she does not have to worry about or manage her condition
alone. When she comes in for her appointments, we review her
current stressors, her reactions, and different ways of responding. I help her identify old habits and together we discover more
successful solutions to the problems life brings.

Gloria has developed a healthier set of coping strategies. We
work together closely to find the correct dosage of medications
to help her manage her seasonal bipolar flare-ups. She has also
decided to actively overcome the memories that would other-

wise debilitate her. She volunteers at a local hospital, and the regularity and responsibility of this work gives her incentive to conquer her fears. She forces herself to leave her house to go to work even when cold and snowy weather would otherwise tempt her to stay in bed.

It's a different matter when it comes to social engagements. She still frequently cancels plans when she's feeling anxious or frightened, and gives in to the urge to curl up in her warm, safe home. But she now draws upon happy memories to make her feel better. Instead of letting winter trigger bad memories, she tries to fill her life with positive triggers. She has decorated her Boston condo to evoke her happy experiences in the Caribbean, with bright red and orange painted walls, colorful rugs, and lots of tropical prints. She keeps the heat up as high as she likes, and she keeps two sunlamps running to give her home a sunny glow. And whenever she's feeling down, she puts on her favorite reggae music and sashays around a bit.

We continue to enjoy or suffer from a rich encyclopedia of experience because of the way our brains encode, catalog, and elaborately cross-reference events and context. As F. Scott Fitzgerald put it in *The Great Gatsby*, "So we beat on, boats against the current, borne back ceaselessly into the past."[8] In my view, however, we are not going against the current. We move ahead in life, conditioned by our experiences. Our memories serve to remind us of countless lessons learned, with vivid associations in all of our senses. We can shape our future by being mindful of what we have come to expect and then by fashioning our present with what works better for our health and well-being. As Robert Frost reflected, "My aim in life has always been to hold my own with whatever's going. Not against: with."[9] I believe this is good advice for us all. We work with what we have. Thanks to our memories, we have a lot.

10

✐

The Cultural Calendar

[At Thanksgiving] the legacy of the garden, and that
hot summer, sits steaming on a side table. There are the
green beans, cooked to death, with pork, and the corn,
simmered with butter. The tomatoes my Uncle John
threaded his way through months ago are now pickled
in quart jars, bright with dill. . . . Plates overflow. We
drink sweet tea—this is a Protestant house, and the
only alcohol is in the medicine cabinet. Dessert is
pumpkin pies, pecan pies, coconut cake, and a chilled
strawberry shortcake. I almost never eat dessert because
I am never able. I live in big cities, in New York, Los
Angeles, Boston, Atlanta, Miami, so I do not see this
food for the rest of the year. I eat until it hurts.

—RICK BRAGG, "Dinner Rites," *Food & Wine*, November 1999

IN THE UNITED States, Thanksgiving is one of the important, emotionally charged days on the calendar. It brings together families for a menu that pays tribute to the seventeenth-century harvest feast between the Pilgrims and the native people. This day, like many others, falls into a cycle of events and seasonalities that we share. Although you may never have thought about it, your own psychological state is almost certainly linked to seasonal cultural forces, whether you feel a growing dread as Christmas approaches or nostalgia for summers past every Memorial Day. For Emma, the start of the school year is always a difficult time, as is Christmas; while the cause of her trouble is unique to her own experiences, many people have similar anxieties for their own reasons at those times of year.

The emotional patterns that are linked to shared events and seasonalities are what I call our "cultural calendar." This is distinct from your individual emotional calendar, which is related to important events in your own life, such as a birthday or a wedding anniversary. Being aware of your reaction to events on the cultural calendar can help you plan ahead for joyous celebrations, as well as prepare for times that may be fraught with negative associations.

Cultural Calendars Around the World

Throughout history, people all over the world have marked different parts of the year with expected patterns of behavior. Holidays define many of the events on the cultural calendar. There is Golden Week in Japan (April 29 to May 5), when people celebrate a string of national holidays; the weeks from Christmas through January 9 in Russia, when most of the country shuts down and everybody parties; and Qing Ming in China, usually in April, when families welcome spring by tidying the graves of loved ones. There are also days given over to more solemn remembrance, such the anniversary of the Tiananmen Square protests in China; the anniversaries of Pearl Harbor and 9/11 in the United States; the Day of Reconciliation in South Africa, which celebrates the end of apartheid; and many, many more.

While some of these holidays remain conveniently affixed to our own monthly calendar, others can be elusive and irregular. The Jewish and Islamic holidays are marked on a lunar, rather than a solar calendar (such as the Gregorian calendar). Because the lunar calendar does not match the cycle of the earth around the sun, it tends to shift backward over time. So on the Jewish calendar, Rosh Hashanah, the Jewish New Year, might fall on October 4 (as it did in 2005) or on September 9 (as it did in 2010).

The Jewish calendar uses leap years to remain aligned with the seasons (and thus with the Gregorian calendar), allowing for about a one-month variation. Still, the calendar can cause some confusion for people trying to reconcile their religious and secular lives. One friend of mine was born on the 13th of April and the 16th of Nissan—the second day of Passover, a Jewish holiday that prohibits eating leavened foods such as bread. This meant that according to Jewish tradition he was forbidden to eat cake on his birthday, while on the secular calendar there were some years when he could eat cake.

The Islamic calendar has even more variation because it doesn't use a leap year. So, for example, the holy month of Ramadan began on October 4 in 2005, and on August 11 in 2010. This makes a big difference for those who practice Islam. Because Ramadan is a month of purification, Muslims spend that month fasting between sunrise and sunset, eating only after the sun goes down. As a friend recently explained to me, in 2005 this meant that Muslims in Boston had to wait between ten and twelve hours to eat. But in 2010, because summer days are so much longer, they had to wait more than fourteen hours between meals!

An important time of year need not be marked by a holiday or a feast day. Ethnographic studies of the Massa people of northern Cameroon in Africa, for example, conducted by Igor de Garine over a thirty-five-year period, show that the Massa have a specific calendar that includes the types of activities that are best pursued at certain times. For them, December through April is the "merry season." October and November are the best months for "strolling and visiting." House building goes well in March, and sexual activity is most smiled upon from January through May. August and September are characteristically given over to "fattening sessions."[1]

The atoll of Pukapuka is a string of tiny islands in the Pacific Ocean. When anthropologist Ernest Beaglehole described this isolated culture in 1937, the population was only five hundred. Their calendar year was strongly defined by weather patterns, with associated emotions and behavior. The fair season from March to November brought gentle, steady trade winds. It was followed by a season of unpredictable and threatening gales, from November to March, which was defined by anxiety over these impending storms. The end of hurricane season—and of all that built-up social anxiety—gave way to a month of feasting and celebration. "The anxiety and worry of the previous months, during which there was an ever-present danger that each day would be the last, was allowed to drain away through a patterned emotional catharsis," Beaglehole observed.[2] Even after the culture was Christianized, the church largely took over this needed catharsis period, encouraging a three-week period of thanksgiving and prayer followed by raucous dramatic performances drawn from the Bible or traditional island history.

American Cultural Calendars:
The Sports Year

Modern American culture has more than just the four seasons, too. I can't remember the last time I celebrated the harvest, and I don't organize my life around the approach of the first snow. But like most people my life is highly dependent on other kinds of cycles. Politics, sports, psychiatry: they all have their seasons.

The psychiatry cycle really has only two seasons: a long September-to-June workload, with particularly busy periods at intervals throughout these months, and then a period of calm in July and August. It's tempting to split this up into fall, winter, spring, and summer, but that's not accurate: my life in June (summer) is much closer to my life in February than it is to my August holiday. Actually, most professions follow a cycle that doesn't match traditional weather patterns. Although we usually think of teaching as a four-season career, teachers in American public schools work from early August to mid-December and from early January to mid-June. In the school year, "winter" and "summer" are mostly symbols, dividing the year into two parts. As vacations, they last two to eight weeks. And while politics follows an annual cycle, it also cycles in two-, four-, and six-year patterns for politicians and their staff.

Sports seasons have their own patterns of annual repetition. As I discussed earlier, organized sports in America follow complex seasonalities: football lasts from September to February; basketball goes from October to June; soccer extends from March to October; baseball lasts from April to October. Then there are golf and tennis, which are played year-round; the Olympics, which alternate between summer and winter every two years; and the soccer World Cup, which occurs every four years. And that's only to name a few of the thousands of sports—from polo and rugby to table tennis and crew—that occupy people the world over.

For serious sports fans, it is not unreasonable to imagine that these seasons have a great deal more emotional resonance than, say, the summer solstice or the spring equinox. Sports events can define each week, leading to high expectations on Sunday afternoon and joy (or disappointment) on Monday morning. Like more traditional seasons, they also have an internal rhythm. Sports seasons open with a rush of energy and high expectations. In the deep phase, anxiety might rise as teams define themselves for the season and set their course for the championships. As the championship approaches, be it the World Cup, the Super Bowl, or (my favorite) the World Series, enthusiasm and anticipation builds.

For some people, the emotional power of the sports season can actually be detrimental to their well-being. The British comic Alistair McGowan's life revolved around another kind of football—what we Americans call soccer. From 1999 to 2002, McGowan costarred on the BBC's *Big Impression* with fellow comedian and girlfriend, Ronni Ancona. But then the couple split up—because of football. Apparently Ancona felt suffocated by her partner's addiction, while McGowan found himself unable to relate to her less-sports-oriented friends. The problem was so bad that in 2009, after Ancona had married and had children, they reunited to write a book about sports addiction.[3] The book, "part memoir of a football addict, part comedy self-help manual," offers a twelve-step approach to breaking a football addiction. Their methods might not be clinically verifiable but, at least, McGowan claims that they helped him grow as a person.[4]

With so many different kinds of seasons at play, it is not surprising that they interact in complicated ways. Hunter S. Thompson, the unruly hero of sports writers, political writers, and angry counterculturalists alike, was an avid American football fan. In the summer of 2004, as both the football season and the presidential elections approached, he wrote a humorous piece on ESPN.com about the possibility that President Bush would cancel football until after the election.

> Sean Penn called me last night and said he was quitting the movie business until after the football season. . . . His voice sounded strange, so I goaded him.
>
> "The football season has been canceled this year. The White House just announced it."
>
> "No!" he shouted. "That's impossible! Football season will *never* be canceled in America—not in an election year. There would be riots."[5]

Thompson, a self-confessed "football addict," went on to draw parallels between the elections and the football season: two integral pieces of the American cultural calendar. This is a theme he had picked up before: in 1968, he became infamous for agreeing to ride in a limousine with Nixon during the presidential campaign only if Nixon promised to talk exclusively about football.[6]

But it wasn't just about entertainment for Thompson. For sports fans, the end of a season can bring with it a sense of disappointment and loss. Thompson felt this deeply: sarcastic to the last, when he killed himself in February 2005, his suicide note was titled "Football Season Is Over."[7]

But for most of us, the change of seasons can bring hope as well. After all, the end of football season means that spring training and March Madness are just around the corner, and soon baseball season will be in full swing. And then, it's just a few short months before football begins again.

Your Emotional Calendar and the
Cultural Calendar

The standard 365-day paper calendar—the kind we hang on our walls every January—helps us divide time throughout the year. Around the world, these calendars are customized to reflect the cultural markers important to different peoples. This cultural calendar is the backdrop for your emotional calendar. Naturally, your own calendar cannot be laid out with the same precision as an Outlook grid. Yet I have found that the holidays and other culturally important events of the year, such as the anniversary of 9/11, often do coincide with emotional hotspots. This creates an overlap between your cultural and your emotional calendars.

It is because of this overlap that the holidays can be particularly difficult times. If your own feelings run counter to the cultural script—which has often been written with commercial considerations, including marketing and advertising, and by the popular media—you may feel out of sync and out of sorts. For example, the supermarket displays of lemonade, hot dogs, and cupcakes suggest that you are supposed to be having a glorious cookout on the Fourth of July. If summer weather makes you irritable, you may resent the socializing required of such an event, or feel like you're being rude if you skip it altogether.

Changing Our Response
to the Holidays

The dates of the holidays may be fixed on the cultural calendar but our reactions to them do not have to remain static. Just as each of our emotional calendars is different from everyone else's, so, too, do our own calendars change over time. Some things may stay consistent for an entire lifetime, but as we move to different places, accumulate experiences both painful and joyful, and change our views with age and wisdom, our health and behavior throughout the year shift to reflect those changes.

For Greg, the eighty-nine-year-old we met who enjoys his "shack" on Nantucket, the winter holidays changed for him as he grew older. He admitted the holidays were "not great" for him anymore. It's not that he was alone: he went to Thanksgiving and Christmas get-togethers where there were fifteen or twenty people. But still, he reflects, "I just feel as though I'm not part of it, even though I'm at the party. I see many of these people only at holidays and events. And my hearing has gone south, pretty much, so that even with a hearing aid, I don't do too well with that." For him around this time of year, he says, "there's a little gloom."

It turns out that for Greg small family get-togethers are more emotionally satisfying than big staged holiday events. Every Sunday he looks forward to going over to his son's house for dinner, and this has become a "sort of ritual" for them.

Days with powerful emotional charges don't have to be set by the cultural calendar. Finding regular times that have meaning just for you can make these moments the most intensely felt of the year.

Christmas: A Hotspot for Most

Ebenezer Scrooge was not a fan of Christmas and its attendant rituals (until his famous revelation), and many people share his aversion. The English newspaper the *Telegraph* recently published a list of "The 10 Worst Things About Christmas." Singled out for particular scorn were the "damn music," the office party ("essentially the combination of copious free alcohol and your employers in the same room is a bad one"), and the decorations, especially "the vast gaudy stuff that takes over city centres."[8]

The distress associated with Christmas is widespread and concerns many aspects of the holiday. The time can be fraught with the clash between expectations of a happy family gathering and the reality of overspending on presents and delicate negotiations about whose turn it is to host dinner. It's not always easier for people who don't celebrate Christmas at all because they practice another religion. They may find themselves with nothing to do, nowhere to go, and lots of resentment about being left out of a holiday that seems to have overtaken the entire month of December and much of November.

However, many people not only come to terms with Christmas, they find ways to make it a joyous part of their lives. Alice, for example, is eighty years old, has five children and thirteen grandchildren, and lives in the Midwest. She has vivid memories of an idyllic New England childhood spent with her family. At Christmas they went into the woods behind her grandmother's house to collect greens. For Alice, this is what the holiday still fundamentally means to her. "Since Mommy and I didn't bake, Christmas was always about decorating the house with live greens. That was always something fun that we all could do together. And that's still really the big joy of Christmas for me," she says. Alice continues to decorate her home with evergreen garlands today, even though she no longer bothers with a Christmas tree since her children are grown.

Alice loves Christmas, but she is aware that many others do not—including her husband, who, she says, "doesn't like to be told when he has to do something." Curious why other people had such trouble with the holiday, she took a class called "Why I Hate Christmas" at her church. The class was full of women, all stressing out about shopping, cooking, and decorating the house. "Christmas is pretty much women's work," she notes. "There's so much stuff to do, and it's sort of dumped on us."

What did she learn about herself in a room full of people who hate Christmas? Alice realized that she'd spent years worrying about getting all her Christmas cards out on time. "At the end of the class we all said, well, what are we going to not worry about? And I decided that I'm not going to worry about the Christmas cards anymore. If they don't get out on time, well, I'll send a Valentine to everybody. And it really isn't that important. In fact, I have done that and many people have responded immediately and said, 'Oh, we loved hearing from you after the bustle of Christmas.'"

A *Telegraph* reader named Nick posted a response to "The 10 Worst Things About Christmas" article by offering his solution to too many presents. "Christmas is ruined by presents. The faux joy needed, the eager, almost desperate expressions on relative's faces when you unwrap something you don't want. Last year my family had a fantastic Christmas by not buying one another anything at all. It sounds cheap and nasty but without the pretence, everyone relaxed."[9]

The Hallmark Holidays

The commercialization of our national holidays has contributed a good deal to our sense of what a holiday "should" be, and Hallmark has played a major role in shaping the images we have of our most essential holidays. According to its Web site, since its founding in 1910, the Kansas City–based company has helped establish and define the greeting card industry. In 2010, its centennial year, the company was publishing cards in more than thirty languages and distributing them in more than one hundred countries. The top three card-sending occasions are Christmas (1.8 billion cards), Valentine's Day (152 million), and Mother's Day (141 million). Father's Day is in fourth place with 93 million cards sent.[10] Despite the popularity of these holidays, many of my patients experience difficulty when their lives do not match up to the loving images on the cards. Valentine's Day might remind one person of a painful divorce or breakup; Mother's Day might remind another of troubled family dynamics.

For Joanne, forty-nine, Father's Day proved to be a hotspot. Since both of her grandfathers died before she knew them, and her own father and only uncle died before she turned ten, she grew up without any father figures in her family. As the momentum for the day built up with advertisements for ties and fishing lures, Joanne felt nothing but loss. For many years, she simply ignored Father's Day. After her marriage and the birth of her two children, she was no longer able to avoid her feelings. "I knew I should be putting on a happy face for my husband and for my father-in-law, but what I really felt like doing was going up to my room and crying," she said.

Through the yearly ritual of helping her children make cards for their father and their grandfather, and planning special family activities together, she was able to turn the day into a more positive experience. She now understands that nothing will cancel out her own losses, but Father's Day need not be the time to mourn. "I focus on the fathers in my life now so I can celebrate with them," she says.

A New Emotional Hotspot: 9/11

Let's look more closely at an emotional hotspot for many that is especially remarkable for being a recent development in our culture: the destruction of the World Trade Center in New York City on the morning of September 11, 2001. For Cass Collins, who saw both planes go into the twin towers, there is not only the immediate aftermath of the event—for her, akin to ASD— but also many repercussions that echoed years later. The event changed her emotional calendar forever, becoming almost a dividing line in her life. At the same time, each passing anniversary brings different echoes, continually surprising her in the way the memories clearly remain alive in her mind.

Cass lives in the Tribeca neighborhood in New York City. She's in her late fifties, with red hair and an "I get it" sense of humor that lights up her face. A former advertising executive, she left the corporate life when her children were young and started a playgroup in her funky downtown loft. Now that her children are grown she spends more time at her country house in Delaware, where she writes a column for the local newspaper. She has explored the topic of 9/11 and its emotional aftermath in several of her columns. This exercise has helped her gain perspective on the traumatic events she witnessed.

On the morning of September 11, 2001, Cass set out with her daughter for school. She remembers the weather was beautiful and it was election day in the city. It was her daughter's first day of middle school and the first time she was going to walk there by herself. Cass took her down to the elementary school, and then watched her walk over the West Side Highway overpass to her new school across the highway. "I figured, OK, she's good. She's on her own. It was a big day: sixth grade, a complete change in everything." She watched her daughter's red hair go over the bridge safely.

Cass stopped at the elementary school to greet some parents of children in her playgroup. It was also a big day for many of these families—the first day of kindergarten. She was talking and looking north when she saw a huge plane fly phenomenally low and straight down Greenwich Street. "It was clear to me within an instant that this was not an accident," she recalls. "That this was deliberate. It was going really fast, and it was very low, and for some reason I don't really remember the noise of it. . . . And I just literally saw it go over my head. And in that moment, as it was going over my head and I was looking up into the belly of the plane, I had a very strong sense of all those people in there. A very strong feeling of, 'Oh my God, what they must be going through.'" And then she remembered, "Oh my God, my child is in that school."

She reached the school and was waiting in the playground for her daughter to be brought down when the second plane hit. She saw a large metal object, like an engine, fly out of the plane and fall onto the street. The first tower was burning by this point, lots of red and smoke. By coincidence her husband was at the school because he had been fixing a malfunctioning voting machine there. The family started back to their loft. At one point, she looked back—and then, following her lead, so did her young daughter. "[It was] a mistake," she remembers. "Because then we saw people falling from the building. Or jumping, I guess, we now know, jumping from the buildings. And they looked more like sticks, really. But they were people. And so that was pretty shocking." Her daughter still remembers the sight, though she didn't talk about it for a long time.

That evening, Cass says she had already noticed an emotional change that would stay with her long after the event. They went out to dinner, "and I can remember ordering a cheeseburger. . . . I had been very good about my diet. And I consciously said, like, to hell with it. The world's falling apart and I'm going to freaking have a cheeseburger if I want one. And I sort of saw that as a change in attitude about the world in that moment. Sort of like, there are things to worry about and there are things to worry about." In general, she became more careless about her health. "I think because I felt less in control," she reflects. "It occurred to me that my best efforts were really for naught."

The year continued to be emotionally difficult for her: her mother, who was in a nursing home at the time, stopped eating the day after 9/11—though it probably wasn't connected. She died in late November. Cass slipped into a depression that she describes as "a kind of affectless behavior." She noticed an inability to do things that she used to be able to do easily, such as make dinner for her family or manage the household. She did reopen her playgroup in October of that year, "but it became clear to me that that was going to be my last year because of the enormous responsibility, all of a sudden, that I felt for having those children there. I just didn't want to deal with it anymore."

She vividly remembers the day of the first anniversary of 9/11 in 2002. She and her husband went down to Battery Park and sat together on a bench. It was another beautiful day, but she remembers there was a fierce wind. "And it felt unmistakably to me like thousands of souls. It was this kind of temperatureless wind. It wasn't cold, it wasn't hot. It was just persistent." Her husband held her and they sat looking at the river. "Feeling almost indescribable feelings," she recalls. "Just emotion. And then being very glad that day was over."

The anniversary is still emotional for Cass, "but it's not at all what it was like for many years." She has been helped by counseling and medication. She still always takes time to honor the day in some way. She tries to be conscious of taking care of herself around that day, and not making too many demands on herself.

Last year, though, right on the anniversary, something occurred that told her that she's still not past the memories.

She was in the country and took a bike ride with her dog. She was holding on to the leash and the bike handlebars at the same time. Suddenly, the dog lunged at a squirrel. Cass went over the handlebars and landed on her head. She got knocked out for a moment and was badly bruised and shaken. "It did occur to me then, wow, this is really weird. I did this to myself on September eleventh. I guess I wasn't feeling as steady as I thought I was. I had been so proud of myself. 'Oh, look at me, I'm not wallowing in self-pity' or, 'I'm not feeling scared' or anything like that." Another year on the anniversary she decided to chop down a tree in the country—and a branch fell down on her head! She says she feels a kind of "get-out-there" urge on the day, which sometimes ends badly. She also worries still about the long-term health effects of 9/11 exposure, so that "every time I have a cough or something I worry about lung cancer."

She notices that 9/11 has eclipsed another cultural event that used to mark the fall season for her: the assassination of President John F. Kennedy on November 22, 1963. "That day could never come without me thinking about it, because it was kind of the first time that the world turned upside down in my lifetime."

There are so many things happening in Cass's story: a broadly shared cultural event; three personal milestones (her direct experience of the bombings as well as its intersection with her daughter's first day of middle school and her mother's declining health); and searing environmental triggers (the beautiful day painfully mismatched with the event, and then, a year later, the haunted wind).

Even for someone as aware as Cass is of what she went through, the anniversary continues to surprise her with—literally—bonks on the head. Next year, she thinks she may just curl up and read a book on that day.

Happier Hotspots on the Cultural Calendar

Western researchers have focused a lot on winter holiday stress and depression, particularly around Christmas and New Year's Day. We've seen how Brian used to bottom out during the holiday season with family tensions followed by binge drinking. But not all spots on the cultural calendar have negative associations. We need to remember that emotionally charged times can be positive and energizing for us as well, giving us a zing that propels us along. Consider Alice, the eighty-year-old who likes to celebrate Christmas. She is someone who has an uncanny understanding of her emotional calendar, though she doesn't call it that, and who has led an enviably joyful and mindful life. Just talking with her is like being sparked with energy, and it's hard not to feel uplifted by her spirit. She talked us through the year in her memory, explaining how she pictures her calendar as a sort of circular plate marked by the various seasons, holidays, and personal events that have defined her life.

As a child, Alice found that the cycle of her year was strongly connected to the flow of the four seasons. The snowy winter flowed into wet spring, as she and her brothers broke up the melting ice on their driveway. Her memories of early spring are close to perfect: "Spring is when you get on your bike and you leave your coats and hats and mittens at home. The wind blows through your hair and you can ride your bike to school. And Mommy starts to get out in the garden. It's all very exciting." She speaks in the present tense, as if it is all still alive in her mind.

Every summer, the family went to an island off the coast of Maine. The ritual of going there was the same each year: "The last day of school we would get our report cards. Mom and Pop would be outside the school door waiting to receive the report cards. And once those had been read we hopped in the car, which was packed for the entire summer."

The family would picnic on a rock on the way to Maine, arriving at the island at supper time. Her memories of the final approach are all drama and fun: "You cross three bridges to get to our island, and after the second bridge there is a very steep hill. This was back in the thirties, you know, when the cars and the roads were not very good. And Pop would say, 'Oh, I don't think I'm going to make it up this hill!' He'd say, 'Help me!' and we'd all flap our arms. 'We're helping, go, go!' And we'd finally hit the bridge to our island and we'd all scream."

The island life was a mixture of total freedom with sailing, rock hopping, and swimming—"we wore out two pairs of sneakers a summer, and we never had to take a bath"—and daily order. "Mommy had a horn that she would blow at quarter to twelve so we'd be in for lunch at twelve o'clock sharp, and have dinner at six o'clock sharp."

Returning to school was the worst part of the year for Alice, because she had to leave the island. "It was so sad. But we were brown as berries. And we would go to school the first day, and there would be all these pale kids. They'd had to spend the whole summer playing under the shade of the elm trees."

Alice's mother once told her they took the children to Maine to "fill you up with health." Alice feels that the health she was filled up with during those summers of her childhood lasted not only through winter but throughout her adult life.

"My life has been a beautiful journey," she says. I wonder how many of us will say that at her age?

11

⁓

Your Personal Calendar

The woods are lovely, dark and deep.

But I have promises to keep,

And miles to go before I sleep,

And miles to go before I sleep.

—ROBERT FROST, "Stopping by Woods on a Snowy Evening"

THIS IS ONE of my favorite poems. What I like about it is that while the poet stops in the dark, snowy woods and seems to get almost hypnotized by their silence, he remembers some mysterious promises that only he knows about. For some reason we'll never know, he has miles to go before he sleeps. Some sense of personal meaning drives him on, at odds with the countryside filling up with snow. For me, this poem is about charting your own course, about knowing yourself and what you need to do.

This chapter is about something similar: it's about the days and milestones that have meaning only to you, that define your personal life experiences, your private calendar. You may share these personal days with your circle of friends and family, but society as a whole takes no particular notice. Your birthday or the anniversary of the death of someone you loved are examples. Or, perhaps, the day you find out a child is on the way, and then the day that child is born.

These personal calendar days can overlap with those on the larger cultural calendar, as, for example, when Emma's boyfriend told her on Christmas that he had never loved her. Or when Cass's mother stopped eating the day after the 9/11 attacks. Whether welcome or miserable, these are the most intimate days of your emotional calendar because they are individual to you.

For this reason, you will probably find these are some of the most emotionally charged days of your year.

Birthdays: A Frequent Hotspot

In the world of astrology, the day of your birth foretells your future. From your character traits to your relationships and career path, astrologers say that your secrets lie in the stars that shone the day you were born. In the world of the emotional calendar, the day of your birth is also potent.

As children, we are taught to treat this annual event as a day of celebration. We mark the day with balloons, gifts, and parties. We bring cupcakes to school and sing special songs. But things get more complicated for adults. "Dissonance" is a word that describes what we experience when our emotions are different from the way that we are expected to feel. The term comes from music: a lack of harmony in sounds. This lack of harmony is revealed when, for example, we feel sad during the holidays, or maybe gloriously alive in February. On a birthday, this out-of-sync feeling is made more poignant by the fact that the expected emotion is exclusive to you. A sad birthday, if it happens, can feel like a personal failure.

Maybe this is why the theme of birthdays gone wrong resonates with so many people. In the second *Twilight* movie, *New Moon*, for example, a happy birthday party becomes a dramatic turning point. On Isabella Swan's eighteenth birthday, her vampire lover, Edward Cullen, and his vampiric family throw her a party. But while unwrapping a gift Bella gets a paper cut. The scent of her blood throws one of the family members into a frenzy, and he attacks Bella. Boyfriend Edward steps in and saves her, but the incident makes him realize just how dangerous it is for Bella to spend time with the Cullens. He breaks up with her, and the family moves away, leaving Bella devastated and depressed. Talk about a weird date on Bella's emotional calendar!

YouTube lists almost five thousand videos on birthdays gone wrong, while a Google search yields more than sixty-five million hits. Online threads reporting sad birthdays abound, such as one on answers.yahoo.com requesting "sad birthday quotes" for an upcoming party.[1] On another thread, a mother writes sorrowfully, "[My daughter] has a birthday coming up. I invited her entire brownie troop (13 girls) and her entire class (19 students). NO ONE, not one is coming. Most didn't have the decency to RSVP, so I emailed and or called them all. They all have a 'thing' to attend. I am so pissed off I don't know what to do. There will be family there but no children. My daughter is 6."[2]

On another thread on answers.yahoo.com, a girl wrote, "I'm turning 13 on November 23. And I am very upset. I have been crying but when my family asks me 'Are you excited!?' I just smile and look down and say 'Yes, I am.'" She adds, "Sometimes I think I have no reason to live, because in a week I'll be a stupid teenager, not a little kid."[3]

This poor girl may be getting ahead of herself, but there's no doubt that birthdays are emotionally charged markers in how we track time. One man I know, Tom, designed a contest for his fiftieth birthday for guests to guess how many places he had lived in his life. The answer? Twenty! Because he has successfully adapted to living in places as diverse as New York and California, the Midwest and France, this was an opportunity for him to look back and feel some pride about his accomplishments and a well-lived life.

But some of us work very hard to do the opposite: ignore the track of time. There's a funny line in the song "Bosom Buddies" from the musical *Mame*. Mame asks, "How old are you, Vera? The truth!" and then follows up with, "I'd say somewhere between forty and death!" As we get older and our relationship to our age shifts, we may come to see our birthdays as yearly reminders of our own diminishing looks, frustrated dreams, and inevitable mortality. This can cause us to dread our birthdays and try to avoid them, but they're there, lurking on the calendar nonetheless.

Celebrating your children's birthdays can go a long way toward bringing back some of the joy we experienced with our own birthdays when we were younger, but they can also obscure how we feel about ourselves. Linda, for example, who got Lyme disease on her birthday and lost the magical feelings she had associated with the day, goes a little crazy each year on her daughter's birthday in February.

"We start planning by Christmas," she says. "One year we had a tropical party for twenty-five kids that was really more like a carnival. We had mock surfing, make-your-own volcanoes, hairdressers doing dreadlocks, a chocolate fountain. Every year we overspend. This year we took all her friends for tea at the fanciest hotel in the city. I guess I just want her birthday to feel magical. But my own? I just wait for it to be over."

Birthdays are personal "zings" on your emotional calendar that recur in a steady pattern. If nothing else, we can expect them. But some zings are more like random bolts of lightning, after which nothing is the same.

Seasonal Dislocation

Not all personal hotspots occur at times of particular significance on our calendars, such as our birthdays or the anniversary of tremendous events. Sometimes an apparently minor episode can trigger the same feeling of being out of sync or out of sorts that a recurring hotspot does.

One of the most prevalent and complicated of these influencers is a phenomenon I call "seasonal dislocation": a feeling of being out of touch with the current season or longing for a different season than the one we're in. We've all experienced this at some point in our lives: you wake up and smell a certain something in the air that makes it feel like spring, even though it is February, and all day you simply feel different. Bashō, the Japanese poet, expressed his sense of seasonal dislocation in this haiku:

> *First day of spring—*
> *I keep thinking about*
> *the end of autumn.*[4]

The sense of dislocation may also come over you when you watch a Christmas movie on television in mid-June. You suddenly crave hot cocoa, and the summer heat and the thought of going to your son's softball game seem unbearable. The feeling is usually fleeting, lasting only a few minutes or up to a day, but it can have a serious impact on the way you think and act during that time, as well as how you remember those moments later on.

Seasonal dislocation is especially acute in these modern times of climate change and long-distance travel. Frequent travelers, especially, often get a strong sense of dislocation that can make them react in a variety of ways: feeling cranky, dull, or even giddy. We feel jet lag not just because our internal clocks are out of alignment with the time zone we're in, but also because we feel out of place with the environmental conditions.

Consider your own work environment. If you're like millions of people who work indoors, your climate is probably pretty much the same from season to season. In fact, the designers and managers of office buildings, hotels, malls, manufacturing facilities, and other large buildings and workplaces pride themselves on achieving a virtually neutral environment where the light levels, temperature, and air circulation are always the same. While technology has no doubt made us more comfortable, this rather artificial sense of homeostasis also causes many of us, myself included, to experience seasonal dislocation.

Another cause of this feeling can be a change in your emotional calendar: your perception of a season changes, and so your response to it changes as well. It can be difficult to recognize this change and then to come to terms with it, so people with this type of dislocation can be left feeling anxious, isolated, or sad.

Marie, for example, spends as much of her free time in the summer as she can with her parents, who visit her from Florida. For most of her adult life, summer has been a joyous time for her, and many of her favorite memories are of enjoying her parents' company while they are in the area. In the past few years, however, she has begun to feel sad and even depressed toward the middle of summer. She feels anxious, trying to get as many summer activities in as possible before fall comes, and she feels that summer is never as long or as fun as it used to be. "I can already feel the sadness and a denouement," she said at the end of July, "that it's all starting to come to an end. And there's this little panic in the air that we have these two or three weeks in the early part of August. Everybody is trying to cram in as much as possible."

Marie feels alone in her disenchantment, because she notes that everyone else around her continues to be energized and lighthearted throughout the summer. And now she feels even more isolated because she has discovered the reason behind her change of perception and doesn't want to share it with her family: as her parents get older, she fears that every summer might be the last she gets to spend with them. The feeling was particularly acute this year: "We had a death in the family that prevented us from doing a lot of things that we would have done. So I'm really feeling like we missed summer, we just missed it. Now I'm racing against the clock, because the end of summer is around the corner and I wonder if we're going to make it to next summer."

Seasonal dislocation can be distressing, but it can also offer a new perspective and give you a chance to reevaluate the way you spend your time during that season. A significant change may be necessary to restore your feelings of ease.

Jim: Phone Calls That Change Your Life

Many of the most influential hotspots on our personal calendars have their roots in specific, out-of-the-ordinary events in our lives.

Jim, age forty-seven, went to work as he would on any typical day on November 11, 2003. His public relations firm is based in New York City, where he also lives. "I went to a business breakfast, came back in the office around eleven thirty or noon, and I heard my secretary on the phone saying, 'Who? Who is this? What? What?'"

When Jim picked up the phone he heard his father, barely able to speak, say that Jim's eleven-year-old nephew, Zach, had been struck by a car and killed. Jim's brother, David (the boy's father), had suffered head injuries from the accident and was in the hospital.

Jim, who up to this point had not experienced any major losses or traumas in his life, remembers saying to himself, "I don't know how to deal with this. I don't know what to do. I wish I could just run away." Jim had given up smoking years before, but he remembers going downstairs in his office building and buying a pack of cigarettes. "I actually felt my brain chemistry change that moment when I went downstairs. Everything was awful."

Jim's staff helped him book a flight to San Francisco. He got through the hours by consuming several capsules of Tylenol PM washed down with at least three vodkas. Soon after Jim arrived he went to view Zach's body, a decision he regrets. "I saw it for a glimpse and I had to turn around and walk out. I wish I hadn't, actually. I don't need that image in my mind." Another image that haunts Jim is the chalk outline of Zach's body in the street. The accident occurred right outside his brother's home, as father and son were stepping into a crosswalk to catch a bus. A car came careening up the street, veered onto the sidewalk, and plowed into them. "Apparently, my brother kept saying, 'Stop, stop, stop,' and the car still ran over them," says Jim, still visibly shaken.

The child's sudden death marked a horrendous period for Jim and the rest of his extended family. David and his wife also had a younger boy, three years old at the time. David made a nearly complete recovery from his head injuries, but in the weeks and months that followed, his wife attempted suicide several times, and the marriage broke up. Jim made several trips from New York to San Francisco to try and help.

Jim's personal situation—he is a gay man without children of his own—helped him cope in certain ways. "It was dreadful for me, but it was not my child. It was my nephew. I feel like of all the people in the family, I had the most resources to deal with it, because I was one step removed." Still, he says, "I always felt like there was a puzzle in front of me that I just could not put together. It became very frustrating. For a long time, every time the plane would land in San Francisco, I felt like I was landing in hell."

On the first-year anniversary of Zach's death, the family got together for the unveiling of the tombstone. Six years have now passed, but November 11 remains a difficult date for Jim each year. "I get a feeling of dread around the beginning of November—like 'Oh my God, something really bad is going to happen during this time.' It doesn't last that long, but there's increased anxiety. I feel a little unfocused, unproductive, in a steely, gray haze. And I drink more during this period, which contributes to a little bit of depression," Jim says.

To deal with his feelings, Jim has undergone psychotherapy and also takes antidepressants. One year, he thought he might stop taking his medication in the fall until his therapist reminded him that November was coming. "You can't discount these events and the anniversaries of them. They are significant, and you have to prepare for them and know they're going to happen," says Jim.

As hard as it is, Jim says, it's important to remember the tragedy. What has changed over time for him is knowing that the bad feelings will also pass. Many positive things have happened since the accident. Jim, who was involved in a long-term relationship that broke up after the accident, has a new live-in partner. Jim's brother David has remarried, and his younger son, now nine years old, is thriving. David's ex-wife also remarried. "The younger son has had his issues because of the divorce, and he will always be the boy whose brother died," Jim says. "That will define his life. But he's doing great." David and his new wife are expecting a baby, and Jim and his partner are thinking of adopting a child. "I feel like this is to make up for the loss a little bit. There's obviously no replacement for Zach, but I think that my brother's new baby, assuming everything goes well, and mine, if my partner and I are able to pull this off, will be rejuvenating. I think we've all been thirsty for something rejuvenating in our family for a long time."

Lauren: Healing Through the Year

Jim's story, as devastating as it is, ends with some signs of hope. Scarring events on your emotional calendar, as we also saw with Cass after 9/11, can start to heal over time. We can follow that thread of healing even more with Lauren.

Lauren is an elegant and serene woman who enjoys quiet order in her life. Yet she experienced an incredible pileup of personal events in late 2008: her husband of almost thirty years, Rob, had a stroke the day after Christmas. Her mother died the next day. That Monday, Lauren turned sixty. Two weeks after the stroke Rob died. Those events are still raw in her memory, as you can imagine. Her grief is not yet something she's ready to "let go of" (a term she says she can't stand), but her struggles demonstrate ways we can all cope—and, even better, create positive meaning for ourselves—even while we relive sad events on our emotional calendars.

Rob was an artist of some reputation, and Lauren had been his studio assistant for most of her career. They had no children together, and their world was entirely wrapped up in each other. He called her his "sunshine," and she feels that he brought out the best in her by making her feel unconditionally loved. Even though Rob was seventeen years older than Lauren, she confesses she never pictured life without him.

After his death, Lauren (unconsciously at first) began creating a collection of what she calls "organics." These were once-living things somehow linked to Rob and her memories of him. The collection started after his burial, when she pulled out all the roses from the floral arrangements that had decorated his studio during his celebration-of-life ceremony. She placed them in a glass bowl on a credenza in her dining room, and so began an altar of sorts to her beloved husband.

Rob's birthday came up in early March. Around this time she went to Cape Cod to be with friends. "That morning I sat outside, bundled up on one of the beach chairs," she says. "I just needed the sun. There was a beautiful garden filled with dried hydrangeas. A single white flower caught my eye. It kind of danced along in the breeze, moving closer to me, and then going back, and then coming closer again. For whatever reason, that lonely little one—none of the others were moving, I don't know why—spoke to me. So I went and I grabbed it." She added it to her collection on the credenza.

Another organic addition was especially powerful. Lauren had bought some potted roses for her terrace. She picked out one to memorialize Rob, because the variety was called "Heaven on Earth." By early October, the roses had stopped blooming. Their wedding anniversary that month was approaching. That week, Lauren looked outside and on the rosebush she associated with Rob there was one fat bud. "I clipped it and brought it in," she remembers. "And it was in full bloom on the day of our anniversary. It was like, Rob, you knew I needed roses from you." She added that rose to her collection.

As time went by, however, this shrine began to trouble Lauren. "As December approached, I thought, you know, these have been comforting and company to me, but they're getting dried and old and dusty. What am I going to do?"

She thought about burning the collection and casting the ashes out to sea, but this didn't feel right because she was powerfully attached to these things. Rob had been a painter, and one day the word "pigments" popped into her head. "I said, 'I know what I'm going to do! On the day before the anniversary of his death, I'm going to take each one of them and, with my hands or with a rolling pin, crush them until they're almost powder. Then, in the spring, when the ground is thawed, and it's a beautiful sunny day, I'm going to work them into the soil around Rob's grave.'" Her idea was that the crushed organics would color the soil forever.

Lauren carried out her plan. She was surprised how much of the essential oils were released even after so much time. I find it interesting that Lauren experienced the day before the anniversary of Rob's death as the most emotional time for her, rather than the actual date. When the day itself arrived, she found herself newly composed. "To some degree, I had already relived his death the day before. On the official day I just remembered where each of the pigments had come from. How they had meant something to me throughout the year."

Lauren was amazingly sensitive to the significance of various dates as the year went by, and how they were shaping a new emotional calendar for her. But she finds that other people's strong ideas about the official calendar put expectations on her that she's not ready for. She explains that during the first year after her husband's death, her closest friends "called me once or twice a week to check in, to see how I was doing." But as the year went on, "that started to taper off. Being invited over for dinner every other week, that's starting to shift, and that feeling of being taken care of, the consolation, the giving comfort— that one year point is a demarcation. You know, the one year of mourning. And I find that sometimes if I'm still expressing pain, it might possibly begin to move into an area where it's uncomfortable for people. Our culture really does operate on the idea that it's time to get on."

Aging and Your Calendar

Emotional calendars change over time. Seasons and events change, and of course we ourselves age. One of my patients, Thatcher, had a powerful and self-destructive reaction to his changing calendar after he turned fifty.

"Summer just doesn't mean the same thing as it used to," Thatcher, a married executive, sighed to me one day. His two kids were grown and lived in different parts of the country. "When I was a kid, the whole family went on vacation together. My wife and I did the same thing with our kids when they were young. We did something new and fabulous every year."

Thatcher felt nostalgia for summers past but saw no way to regain that feeling. Sure, he and his wife continued to go to their summer home. And every year, he tried to organize a family trip, usually with little luck. Nothing compared to his happy memories of days that were behind him.

Then one winter, Thatcher discovered Internet dating and porn sites. "I've been chatting with some young women online," he told me, "and I'm seriously thinking about trying to hook up with one or two of them this summer. Maybe it will give me the kind of thrill I got as a teenager, when I was chasing girls and getting laid as often as I could."

Later that winter, Thatcher tried one more time to organize a family trip, but it fell through at the last minute. Although he was extremely disappointed, the experience helped him realize that his plans for summer infidelities were probably just as unlikely to bring back the old thrill. He was finally ready to break out of his pattern and forge something new and positive for himself.

We talked about what summer meant to him, and he became much more aware of how deep his associations were. Eventually, he started to accept that he had been trying unsuccessfully to re-create or recapture the old days.

"There's no reason to stop taking time in the summer to do something new or adventurous," I pointed out. "Maybe you could do something by yourself or with friends. Take some different kind of vacation."

For Thatcher, summer had always meant travel and adventure. The answer for him was to change his attitude by redefining what adventure meant. It could no longer be about beachcombing with his young kids, nor could it be about chasing girls and casual sex. But, to his delight, he discovered a whole new type of vacation available to him in what is sometimes called "voluntourism"—combining a trip to an exotic location and some kind of charitable or helping activity.

Now Thatcher looks forward to his summer travels and loves telling his kids about where he has been and whom he has helped. Not only does he enjoy the trips, he has also made lasting friends.

Embracing our emotional calendars as we age doesn't mean

we have to go to the ends of the earth. Greg, who enjoyed spending time each week with his son, found deep comfort and meaning from a simple shaft of sunlight that flooded into his living room each day. This became his favorite room as he grew older. "In the winter, the sun is low, the sun is all the way across the room, but it gives you hope," he explained.

Many things were changing for Greg as he grew older—his hearing, his mobility, his overall health were failing. But he knew he didn't want to leave his beloved home. He didn't want to go to a retirement home or assisted living because, he said, "as far as the sunshine part, you're not guaranteed." Maybe he'd end up with a north-facing window, or maybe a view of a lower building with an asphalt roof. "You have to use the elevator to go outside. It would be different in such a place."

For Greg, life had slowed to the point where a good day was feeling up to a short walk outdoors. His personal emotional calendar had changed profoundly, but he understood and held on to the pieces he needed to stay grounded.

PART IV

Awareness

The year hastens to its close. What is it to me? That I am

twenty-five or fifty-eight is as nothing. Should I mourn

that the spring flowers are gone, that the summer fruit

has ripened, that the harvest is reaped,

that the snow has fallen?

—RALPH WALDO EMERSON, *Journals*, December 28, 1831

The stories of Lauren, Thatcher, and Greg are not only about the power of personal hotspots. They also illustrate the process of change and healing that we all go through over time. Lauren took control of her mourning period by making positive choices about how she would spend powerful anniversaries, such as the day of her husband's death. Thatcher reclaimed a hotspot that was getting hotter than he could handle when he started traveling during the summers. And Greg found ways to access the meaningful elements of his year even as aging imposed new limitations on his lifestyle.

I hope that as you've read this book, you have taken the time to identify your own physical sensitivities and cultural and personal hotspots, and have been able to integrate these different elements to create a more complete story of your life. Perhaps you have been able to identify times in your past when you were unknowingly influenced by a physical factor or by a personal hotspot. I know that working on this book has brought to light some stories for me.

Now I want to discuss some of the ways you can develop more awareness of your emotional calendar and use this new knowledge in positive ways. I have already introduced the concept of adaptive control, which is a way of maintaining balance in the face of all the destabilizing factors that you confront every day. Lauren exhibited adaptive control when she recognized her need to mourn her losses and created a ritual that would help her deal with them. Thatcher exhibited it when he acknowledged his hotspot and found a healthy outlet for his summer energy. In the following pages, I'll guide you through the process of achieving adaptive control yourself and cover some of the tools and practices that you can use to tend to your environment. And I will talk about when it makes sense to look beyond your ability to help yourself and seek help from an outsider.

I've worked with many people over the years as they have developed and grown in relation to their emotional calendars. Making the move from a lack of awareness to much better awareness and finally to adaptive control may seem difficult. I am constantly working to improve my relationship with my own calendar, especially as my daughters get older, my wife and I juggle our busy schedules on two coasts, and my working life becomes increasingly consuming. But I have seen how effective these efforts can be, both for myself and for my patients. They can make it possible to move beyond a dread of the future and a feeling of everyday anxiety. They not only can improve your subjective well-being, they can, with luck and persistence, lead to the possibility of seasonal embrace.

12

~

Looking Outward,
Looking Inward

*I am writing this now as the end of the first year [after
my husband's death] approaches. The sky in New York
is dark when I wake at seven and darkening again by
four in the afternoon. There are colored Christmas
lights on the quince branches in the living room. There
were also colored Christmas lights on the quince
branches in the living room a year ago, on the night it
happened, but in the spring . . . those strings burned
out, went dead. This served as a symbol. I bought new
strings of colored lights. This served as a profession of
faith in the future.*

—JOAN DIDION, *The Year of Magical Thinking*

SEASONALLY RELATED STRESS, of the kind Joan Didion
describes here, can be deeply troubling. When you don't
feel in tune with how other people are experiencing the
season, you can feel isolated or even in conflict with them. You're
up against a force that is continuous, inevitable, and much larger
than yourself. You can't change the season. You can't keep the

school year from starting or the anniversary of a death from coming. You feel kind of out of control.

Most of us respond to our personal emotional disruptions in the same way, over and over again. We repeat a familiar behavior even when we know from past experience that it may not be such a great way to operate. Why? Because familiar habits, even negative ones, help us all feel more in control, and any semblance of control can be comforting.

Julia, the woman with a fear of thunder in chapter 8, developed a series of what she thought of as tricks that comforted her and made her feel a sense of control during thunderstorms. Actually, though, her tricks were bad habits that did not provide her the help she needed. By burying her head in pillows and wearing earplugs when the weather got bad, she was indulging in avoidance—trying to ignore the problem or escape it, rather than finding a solution to overcome it. When she realized that her tricks were not helping her to get any better, she finally turned to a therapist. She was tired of being incapacitated by storms and wanted to gain control over her life. When a member of our research team spoke with her, she said, "The biggest thing I've learned from therapy is that most of my coping skills are actually escapism. The idea behind my therapy is to confront the problem and make myself so used to it that it stops affecting me that way. All those little tricks I learned to cool myself down are actually not helping at all."

What Julia is working on with her therapist—and what I encourage you to try with your own hotspots, both physical and emotional—is what I have been calling "adaptive control." This is the process by which we become aware of the moods and behaviors that result from emotional hotspots, and then take deliberate steps to change or control them. We have to learn to pay close attention to the ways that seasonal issues cause us distress or discord whether physically or emotionally. The impact of our emotional disruptions may be manifested in something as minor as an uncharacteristic remark we make to our friends or kids, or in a bad habit such as drinking too much coffee or over-sleeping. In more serious cases, it can lead to depression, as it did with Gloria, or a struggle with personal demons, like Brian.

Of course, learning to identify such a disruption takes some work, because we can become so used to feeling anxious that we become incapable of recognizing it as anxiety at all. So the first job we have in achieving adaptive control is to pause a moment and bring our awareness into the present moment. Only then can we take note of how we are feeling emotionally and physically.

Turning Off the Autopilot

The first step toward learning to live with our emotional calendar is to turn off the autopilot and recognize both the positive and negative patterns in our lives. Often, we habituate ourselves to discomfort. We believe that our anger is justified, that our sadness is "no big deal," and that our seasonal affect is just "a part of life." This is how Steve responded to the signs that he was traveling too much: by drinking more Diet Coke and scheduling even more meetings. Turning off the autopilot requires taking the time to sort through our feelings and identify the sources of our emotions. It requires pausing in our daily lives and beginning an inner dialogue with ourselves, to consciously recognize the emotions that we are experiencing and the nature of our reactions.

RACHEL: LIVING OUTSIDE HERSELF

Turning off the autopilot is not easy to do. For Steve, it took a life-threatening illness to force him to take a step back. One young woman I know, Rachel, took a rather unusual and quite wonderful approach. She spent an entire year working as an outdoor educator, which forced her to confront the complexity of her relationship with the seasons.

Like most people, Rachel had never before taken the time to stop and think about her relationship with the seasons. In a description of her outdoor year that Rachel wrote for us, she says that winter had always been "an eternal menacing gray sheet of clouds and an endless dirty stretch of icy roads, punctuated by periods of misery, of loneliness, and of despair." Spring, by contrast, was "a season of joy and renewal." These seem like rather typical emotions, but Rachel found that, in fact, they had little to do with the seasons themselves. She described with surprise her discovery of "unexpected pleasures beneath winter's uniform gray," and wrote that, contrary to her expectations, "spring's arrival was marked by a windstorm that sent three pine trees crashing across the road as I walked home from the supermarket."

Discovering nature's inconsistency disrupted Rachel's emotional stability. She could no longer count on the seasons to match her expectations, an experience that initially made her feel out of control. Not knowing what to expect from the weather left Rachel physically and emotionally unprepared—a situation that could have put her in harm's way, living so close to the elements. In fact, by becoming aware of the disconnect between her expectations and reality, Rachel was taking the first step toward moving from harmful patterns to adaptive control. To take the next step, she had to learn to understand the role that these patterns played in her everyday life.

Rachel tells an interesting story about her first camping trip as an outdoor educator. She was responsible for leading her ten twelve-year-old campers on a five-day course, during which they would live outside, cook over a fire, and use the forest as their classroom. As a first-time instructor, she was under a lot of pressure to perform well. It was early spring, it was cold, and it rained continuously for the first three days of the trip. "By Thursday morning, my students and I were cold, disheveled, and exhausted. Then, to our astonishment, the sun came out." It was only with the emergence of the sun that Rachel was able to see how much she had been affected by the rain. "I realized that I had to reevaluate the way I approached physical discomfort. The only way I would achieve stability was by figuring out how to differentiate between the experience of being wet and cold and the feeling of being unhappy. I needed to find a source of pleasure that lasted beyond the good-weather days."

That week, Rachel learned to take her emotional pulse and recognize the factors that influenced her ability to find joy in what she was doing. Working in the outdoors forced Rachel to reach this understanding quickly. For those of us who keep nature at a distance, taking our emotional pulse may require a different, perhaps more deliberate, kind of effort. It is not always obvious that anxiety at work might be influenced by an impending storm, or that a fight with a loved one is coinciding with a hotspot on your seasonal calendar. Often, in fact, we ignore these "coincidences" or even deny them, believing in our ability to compartmentalize—a belief that reinforces the mythology of control.

There are several techniques that can be used to help you develop healthy coping skills. Emma sits under her sunlamp each morning and tries to fill her mind with joy. Steve makes a conscious effort to stay for a few days in each city he travels to, rather than rushing out as soon as his meetings are done, which gives him time to stabilize himself emotionally. Mindfulness practices, a unique combination of Western and Eastern techniques, use meditation and other mental exercises to improve awareness.

Thinking Positive and Visualizing
Your Success

As we work to shut off the autopilot and take our emotional pulse, it's important that we do our best to think positively about ourselves and our situations—especially with regard to the changes we are instituting in our daily lives—just as Emma tries to come up with a smile during her light-therapy session and Steve now finds pleasure in flying his model airplanes. It can be enormously helpful to take a moment to visualize yourself in a predictably uncomfortable situation. Then, marshal new ways to respond, enacting or imagining the better choices you intend to use when confronted with the familiar challenge. This is a technique that is sometimes called "guided imagery." When you envision yourself responding in a positive way, you rehearse in your mind and get stronger and more able to perform as you have planned.

Harvard psychologist George Vaillant has made an exhaustive and well-known study of what makes us happy. He found that contrary to expectations, the determining factor is not the degree of challenges that we face but the ways that we confront the troubles before us. From an epic longitudinal study of Harvard graduates that has been running for more than fifty years, Vaillant identified several categories of defenses that people use to respond to troubles.[1] These categories range from psychotic (paranoia, megalomania) to immature, neurotic, and mature adaptations.

Most people use a combination of neurotic and mature defenses to respond to troubles. Neurotic defenses include intellectualization, or taking a cold, emotionless view of a situation in order to feel in control; displacement; and repression. These responses tend to reinforce negative patterns. By developing our awareness of the emotional factors of our life and increasing our mindfulness in a given situation, we can learn to use mature adaptations, such as self-observation, self-assertion, altruism, humor, anticipation, temporary suppression of impulses, and sublimation (finding positive outlets for feelings).[2]

Attending to the problem at hand—finding a new and better way to respond to a seasonal stressor—ultimately means three things: gaining perspective, seeking support, and rehearsing in your mind. These are interrelated but separate tasks. It is absolutely critical to work on gaining a better view of the problem, but perhaps even more important is talking about it with others. Reach out to select individuals who can offer companionship and strength in difficult times. A member of your family, a close friend, a teacher, a spiritual leader, or a doctor or therapist are good potential sources of this invaluable support. You can gain additional perspective through this process of reaching out. Visualizing yourself succeeding in your new endeavor, anticipating success, and practicing in your mind's eye will then prepare you for your intended action.

Tending to Your Environment

As diverse as the factors that can affect your emotional calendar are, we can divide them into two categories: external and internal. External factors are the physical and environmental factors that disrupt your homeostasis; internal factors are the emotional hotspots on your calendar. Of course, these two categories overlap and influence each other: a physical ailment can become an emotional hotspot, just as a period of mental distress can have an adverse effect on your body.

General lifestyle changes and management strategies can help you reconcile the external and internal destabilizers on your emotional calendar and assuage the worst effects of each, while you embrace those factors that help you to feel your best.

ALYSON: LIVING ENTIRELY WITHIN THE SEASONS

Adaptive control involves being present in your surroundings and being aware of which factors—both external and internal— are affecting you at a given time. In managing external disruptors, this can mean finding ways of enjoying the physical realities of the world around you.

Alyson Ewald embraces the idea of being present in one's surroundings in a deep and unusual way. We first learned about Alyson in a Bates College alumni magazine, and then the research team tracked her down and talked with her at some length on the phone. Unlike most of the other people featured in this book, Alyson does not struggle with any one specific seasonal problem, physical or emotional. Rather, I wanted to include Alyson because she took a rather remarkable approach to living a mindful life, and I hope that her story will offer you a new perspective.

For years, Alyson felt out of step with the world around her. A devoted environmentalist, she frequently felt judged for the steps she took to reduce her carbon footprint. She felt an almost constant sense of cultural dislocation, and living in the cities and then even the suburbs began to feel suffocating. So Alyson decided to do something drastic: she moved out of "civilization" to live and work entirely in nature.

Alyson now lives with her partner, Mark, daughter, Cole, and a small community of like-minded people at Red Earth Farms in northeast Missouri. Red Earth Farms comprises seventy-six acres of hills, woods, ponds, and a creek. The community was formed in 2005 to be "a clear and visible demonstration of a thoughtful and compassionate way to live on this Earth," according to its Web site.[3]

Alyson's upbringing in Vermont was "unconventional from the start," and it laid the groundwork for her eventual decision to turn her back on an orthodox lifestyle. Her parents were back-to-the-landers in the 1970s. "They weren't full-on hippies," Alyson says, "but they were part of that wave of people who moved to the country, bought a piece of land, and learned how to milk a goat and how to plant a garden." It was all new to Alyson's parents, and her mother was excited to be able to supply the family with fresh, local food on the table. Alyson says she "learned at an early age not just how to bake bread, but how to milk a goat, and how to weed a garden, and how to tell when a tomato is ripe."

Alyson was accepted at Bates College in Maine and spent her junior year in Europe, a time that proved to be a turning point in her life. "What happened while I was in Europe was that I learned about all the different cultures that are out there," she says. "There are so many different ways to approach living on the Earth." Traveling with almost no money, she found herself "having to find out what local people ate and how they cooked. It wasn't the typical tourist experience; it was experiencing how people really live."

Alyson likes to push the edge. When she graduated from Bates, she knew she didn't want to find an office job. So throughout the 1990s she worked with various activist groups in Russia, Ukraine, Hungary, and Croatia on issues such as climate change, transportation, and energy. Eventually, she returned to the United States and settled in Amherst, Massachusetts. There, Alyson tried to apply what she had learned in eastern Europe but felt "I was still really different from most of the people around me." She felt connected to the people she was working with at the nonprofit Sacred Earth Network but disconnected from the wider culture. "That disconnection really affects your quality of life," she observes. "I was unhappy. I felt like I was constantly swimming against the current. It was exhausting."

Alyson became aware that this disconnection was a source of unhappiness for her, and that it wouldn't be enough for her to just change jobs or move to a new town. That realization proved to be a major breakthrough for her. She knew she had to take the situation into her own hands and entirely change the external factors that were causing her disenchantment.

Alyson joined an activist community in Missouri called Dancing Rabbit, and from there she and a few friends went on to establish Red Earth Farms. The idea is to support one another's activism and live according to ecological principles. "I felt I'd found my tribe," she writes in her Web site biography. "I realized I desperately needed to be surrounded by folks who share the same ideals and dreams as I do. That's what keeps me sane, gives me energy, and fuels my creative impulses."[4]

Like any mother, Alyson has found it hard to find time to get much done since her daughter was born, but her special lifestyle makes it all the more difficult. Her laundry routine, for example, is quite different from that of the typical American household. It goes like this: position large washtub under the tap. (Water comes from a nearby pond through a gravity-fed system.) Open spigot and run water into tub. Load dirty clothes into tub, then agitate them with an old-fashioned laundry plunger. When clean, feed clothes through a hand-cranked wringer. Empty tub of dirty water, refill with clean water. Repeat agitation and wringing process. Transfer clothes to basket. Lug basket outside. Hang clothes on the line to dry.

Compared to most of us living in twenty-first-century America, Alyson's community is far more attuned to the natural environment. Alyson observes that the mood of its members is often weather dependent. The last few days before we spoke they had experienced a period of beautiful weather. "It's been crystal clear, eighty degrees during the day, sixty degrees at night. Everyone's been sleeping well. They come to meetings saying, 'The weather's great and I'm doing great,'" she said. But then they were dumped with five inches of rain. When that happens and they have to hole up in their small, cramped living spaces, Alyson reports that everyone gets "really grouchy. Everything's getting muddy. Everything gets moldy and mildewed. The kids are freaking out. They're all covered with mud."

When Alyson is asked if she is happy, she says that she is—but like the rest of us, of course, her life is full of challenges. These are mostly connected to living so close to nature: "What do I do when there are raccoons and possums every night in the corn? What do I do when I can't find the tomato hornworms? Or when my partner feels paralyzed because he has so much to do?"

But she feels connected, she says, to other humans and to the planet. "Every day is full of challenges and interesting conversations and close friends and my beloved family." To Alyson it feels like the natural human state to live connected to a cluster of people and to learn together how to live well in that place.

Adaptive control is not about being happy all the time and, as Alyson's story demonstrates, it's not always about handling specific problems on our emotional calendars. Life will always be full of challenges, and there are always aspects of our lives that we find stressful or that are an effort to deal with. The key is to recognize those elements in your life that are recurring problems and, as Alyson did, find a way to steer yourself in a different situation.

Is Connection to the Seasons Part
of Our Genetic Code?

You don't have to attempt Alyson's radical lifestyle change, or live in a tent for a year as Rachel did, to realize that a positive relationship with nature and the seasons can be a powerful force in creating emotional stability.

Biologist Gordon H. Orians considers our attraction to nature to be a "genetic imperative." He sees the human relationship to nature as critical in our evolutionary development. Evolution, he explains, benefits those who "prefer the environments in which they thrive."[5] That preference leads to better health and more offspring. Our genetic memory is a product of evolution stored in the human genome, so in terms of genetics we are not that far away from our hunter-gatherer ancestors, and we continue to be impacted by what Orians calls the "ghosts of environments past."[6]

Orians's take on memory and how it works is slightly different from the one we discussed earlier. He believes that human memory operates on two levels. Decision making is based on a combination of information drawn from ontogenetic memory, which is our memory of our own past, and the genetic memory stored in the human genome. Our genetic memory enables us to appreciate our relationship with nature; our ontogenetic memory, recorded in our emotional calendar, also associates emotional reactions with physical space. In this way, Orians connects the biological influence of our genetic past to the role of nature in our current lives.

Several recent studies in the emerging field of ecopsychology have shown that exposure to nature can reduce anxiety and stress. (Ecopsychology combines research and theory from a number of different fields of study, including environmental philosophy, ecology, and psychology, and explores the relationship between individual health and wellness and the well-being of the planet itself.[7]) Exposure to nature can also increase directed attention, recharging individuals' ability to focus and perform tasks efficiently. When we live mostly indoors, we lose this connection and its associated benefits. Ecotherapy, which is based on ecopsychology, encompasses a number of practices—including horticultural therapy, green exercise, animal-assisted therapy, and wilderness therapy—designed to help people create a reciprocal, healing relationship with nature and thus improve their emotional state and strengthen their cognitive control.[8]

We have seen how identifying physical factors that affect your emotional calendar can be a powerful part of making positive changes in your life. Many of my patients have developed a keen awareness of low points that may occur throughout the year and that may have overwhelmed them with sadness or anger in the past. By learning ways to anticipate them and take positive steps to counteract them, they can avoid or reduce stress and reach out for extra support when they need it. Sometimes, onetime positive actions, such as buying a nice raincoat, reading a book, or taking a trip, can counteract seasonal patterns. To gain even more adaptive control, we can make long-term changes in our habits or our living environments.

Gardening: How Horticulture Helps

Let me confess that I am not a gardener, never have been a gardener, have never kept a garden, and probably will never do so. However, I know that for many people, my wife included, gardening is a wonderful way to make the kind of connection to nature and the seasons that the ecopsychologists talk about. It can also be a superb way to manage difficult times on the emotional calendar.

Author Michael Pollan writes that, from a philosophical standpoint, "it is gardening that gives most of us our most direct and intimate experience of nature—of its satisfactions, fragility and power."[9] For many, to garden is to become especially aware of our memories, seasonal moods, and feelings associated with the natural environment.

The mental health benefits of gardening have been intuitively understood, no doubt, for centuries and certainly long before the term "mental health" was coined. Robinson Crusoe, for example, is the famous fictional hero of Daniel Defoe's novel of the same name, first published in 1719. Crusoe is castaway on a desert island, the only one to survive a shipwreck. He lives there for twenty-seven years, many of them without any human company, before he is found and makes his way home to England. It's interesting to note that Crusoe does two things, relevant to our conversation, that help keep him sane during all those years spent by himself. One, he sets up a large wooden post to serve as a calendar. "Upon the sides of this square post I cut every day a notch with my knife, and every seventh notch was as long again as the rest, and every first day of the month as long again as that long one; and thus I kept my calendar, or weekly, monthly, and yearly reckoning of time."[10]

Two, he gardens. Yes, of course, he had to, in order to live, but he also found pleasure in it. "I dug up a piece of ground near my new bower, and sowed the rest of my seed in February, a little before the vernal equinox; and this having the rainy months of March and April to water it, sprung up very pleasantly, and yielded a very good crop. . . . By this experiment I was made master of my business, and knew exactly when the proper season was to sow, and that I might expect two seed-times and two harvests every year."[11] Becoming master of one's own business by creating a garden and feeding oneself is a fine example of adaptive control.

Since the early twentieth century, gardening has been prescribed as an intervention for patients at mental hospitals. "Large parks and vegetable and flower gardens were created and maintained by the patients," writes Ingrid Soderback, a Swedish occupational therapist, in a review of the history of horticultural therapy.[12] But, she writes, the notion that garden work "helped patients to feel the rhythm of each day and understand how the garden and gardening shifted during the seasons . . . was more or less abandoned between 1960–1980." The reason for decreased focus on the healing powers of gardening: the rise of psychopharmacology.

During the 1980s, the term "horticultural therapy" (essentially the same as ecotherapy) became more common in the health sciences. A significant body of scientific literature has addressed the issue of horticulture and health, but mostly focused on specific benefits to physical health in cases of chronic or life-threatening diseases. Cognitive benefits are more challenging to pin down but have been shown to include enhanced mood, reduced arousal, and improved concentration. For many, such as gardening expert Ruth Page, gardening is also fundamentally about hope: "The very action of planting a seed in the soil requires hope; by encouraging and in some senses almost imposing a sense of hope onto someone, a personal journey may begin."[13]

One recent study attempted to assess whether "gardens and gardening activity may offer a key site of comfort and a vital opportunity for an individual's emotional, physical and spiritual renewal."[14] The study focused on a group of thirty men and women aged sixty-five to seventy-nine living in a "deprived

area" in northern England. Residents expressed feeling threatened by their immediate environment. The participants were
given one of two local sites to garden as well as full-time support by a qualified gardener. Data were gathered over a nine-
month period through interviews and diaries. It was found that
the "domestic garden is valued by older people as offering a
secure place, away from the perceived threats of the wider urban
landscape, that can be experienced in both active" (i.e., actual
gardening) "and passive ways" (i.e., a place to relax and interact
socially, especially for those with declining physical fitness).[15]
One gardener, Avril, observed about her moods: "I think if I
hadn't had that [the garden] to look forward to I'd have been
much more depressed and weary than I've been. . . . It's been
my main activity since I've had to give things up since being
limited."[16]

New England garden designer Jane Rupley has also observed
the healing possibilities of gardens for herself and her clients.
For her, it's "a little bit of an escape. There's something about
digging in the ground and moving things around and making
something that wasn't there before."[17] She says it's helped her
through some of the most difficult times in her life, and has
helped many clients to achieve the same sense of release with
their own gardens. One of her clients asked Rupley to design a
garden that would be wheelchair accessible so she and her husband, who had been incapacitated by a stroke, could enjoy it
together. "It's an outlet for her," explains Rupley. "She has a husband in a wheelchair. It's got to be just wonderful for her to get
away without going too far. She said to me, 'We can't travel, so
I put everything into the garden.'"

National Public Radio's Ruth Page recounts a humorous
story about her own healing in the garden. She describes a day
when everything went wrong: she forgot about a dentist appoint-

ment; the clothesline broke and her sheets blew all over the yard; she burned plum jam on the stove.

"Forget it," she said. "When three things go wrong by mid-morning, there's only one thing to do. Head for the garden. The beans needed weeding. Great: something to work out my resentments on. I knelt and started; the lamb's quarters and pigweed pulled out easily, so I ripped them out angrily, in big handfuls. That felt good. After a few minutes I was enjoying the comforting feel of the soft, warm earth. . . . As the weed heap grew and the row of handsome, weed-free plants extended behind me, I realized I wasn't frowning anymore; actually, I was smiling. Is gardening therapeutic? You bet it is."[18]

Even though the flowers are dead and the ground is frozen, winter can still be a particularly "ripe" time in a gardener's mind. "I dream of flowers," notes lifelong gardener Alice Church, "although never in the summertime, just in the winter."[19] Michael Pollan writes, "Winter in the garden is the season of speculation, a time when the snow on the ground is an empty canvas that invites the idle planting and replanting of countless hypothetical gardens between now and spring thaw."[20]

EATING: FOOD FROM THE SEASON YOU'RE IN

Since the days of cave dwellers, humans have fed themselves according to the seasons. At first, they hunted and gathered whatever was available. Later, they settled in to raise crops and farm animals. Farming provided the major source of sustenance in the early days of the United States. Over the course of the twentieth century, however, Americans became more and more divorced from the original sources of the food they ate. Innovations in shipping, such as refrigerated boxcars, meant that food could travel farther and farther from producer to table. Thanks to air freight, consumers who can afford the prices now have access to a year-round supply of strawberries, grapes, blueberries, and lettuce, all once available only during limited times of the year.

The instinct to increase and optimize the food supply seems, not surprisingly, to be a fundamental part of human nature. George Washington, who owned and managed a large farm at Mount Vernon, Virginia, for far longer than his tenure as president, dreamed of America becoming the "granary" of the world through wheat cultivation.[21] In *Can You Trust a Tomato in January?* Vince Staten writes, "Man has always tinkered with his food, trying to find ways to preserve it, make it taste better, make it cook faster. . . . As the years have passed, humans have worked on ways to improve on the natural food supply. They have developed hardier, more disease-resistant strains of vegetables, bred larger fruits, and created varieties of grains with larger yields." He facetiously draws "a straight line, if a long one, from the caveman's curdled dinosaur milk to the forever-fresh miracle food called Cheez Whiz."[22]

With all of these technological advances in the food supply, many people are becoming concerned about the prevalence of out-of-season food. Not only is the amount of energy it takes to ship produce around the world environmentally harmful, they argue, it is also ruining the basic pleasure of eating fresh, locally raised plants and animals. Slow Food is a movement that was founded in Italy in 1986 to provide an alternative to fast-food culture. It has spread its operations to one hundred countries since then. In the United States, the main headquarters in Brooklyn, New York, maintains links with two hundred chapters around the country. Slow Food encourages people to get back to seasonal food as a way to connect to nature and appreciate food more. Not only does the group raise public awareness through dinners and educational programs with chefs and farmers, it also promotes "the celebration of food as a cornerstone of pleasure, culture, and community."[23] Through its "Ark of Taste," Slow Food keeps track of foods that are "threatened by industrial standardization, the regulations of large-scale distribution and environmental damage," in an effort to preserve them.[24] Since 1996, it has listed more than eight hundred products in more than fifty countries.

In many restaurants, chefs have committed themselves to following the growing cycle, crediting farmers as the source of their food, and featuring seasonal products. Nationwide, the Chefs Collaborative network helps connect chefs to local sources of food and promotes sustainable food in the culinary community. The group holds workshops and distributes publications such as "Cooking with Heirloom Beans." Its vision is both lofty and simple: "As a result of our work, sustainable practices will be second nature for every chef in the United States."[25]

For individuals, eating food that is in season seems to carry psychological benefits along with incomparably fresh flavors. Author Barbara Kingsolver moved with her husband and two daughters from Tucson to Virginia to grow and eat food produced as close to their farmhouse as possible. She chronicles their year in her book *Animal, Vegetable, Miracle*. "We wanted to live in a place that could feed us: where rain falls, crops grow, and drinking water bubbles right up from the ground."[26] In Tucson, "virtually every unit of food consumed there moves into town in a refrigerated module from somewhere far away," she writes. "Like many other modern U.S. cities, it may as well be a space station as far as human sustenance is concerned."

At its essence, eating local food promotes mental and physical stability. "A food culture is not something that gets *sold* to people. It arises out of a place: a soil, a climate, a history, a temperament, a collective set of belonging. . . . People hold to their food customs because of the *positives*: comfort, nourishment, heavenly aromas," says Kingsolver.

Not every aspect of the Kingsolver experiment went smoothly. The family impatiently endured wind, cold, and mud while waiting for their first spring crops to be ready. Though they successfully grew many vegetables in the warm months, by January their larder had dwindled to legumes, winter squash, and whatever they had stocked in the freezer. The author named February the "Hungry Month." Still, they learned a deep lesson. Tying family meals to the seasons "did acquaint us in new ways with what seasons mean, and how they matter. The subtle downward pulse of temperatures and day lengths created a physical rhythm in our lives, with beats and rests: long muscles, long light; shorter days, shorter work, and cold that drew us deeper into thoughts and plans."[27]

It is this connection to the earth and the natural cycles that seems to ground people who grow their own food. Like the gardeners described earlier in this chapter, vegetable growers seem to find both pleasure and optimism when it's time to plant. Verena Wieloch, a farmer at the Gaining Ground organic community farm in Concord, Massachusetts, writes in the introduction to the group's cookbook, *The Gaining Ground Table*, "Farmers hear the call of spring. We know it through a certain yawning desire for soil underneath the fingernails and the slow, wet smell of a greenhouse. I have yet to meet the one who starts the chain of spring's arrival, but I know what needs to be done: cabbages, spinach, onions, turnips, radishes, and lettuce. Turn over the beds and warm the soil."[28]

The work of growing one's own food creates a multiplier effect: it is good for body, soul, and planet. As essayist and poet Wendell Berry, a champion of local agriculture who published extensively on the subject in the 1960s and 1970s, put it, "A garden gives the body the dignity of working in its own support. It is a way of rejoining the human race."[29]

Decorating: Creating a Pleasing
Interior Environment

The earliest communities of humans survived in caves, tepees, grass huts, and other primitive structures. The function of today's homes—to provide a shelter against the elements—remains essentially unchanged, but in most Western nations, homes have also become a form of self-expression. From paint colors to carpet patterns, every detail of a home reflects an owner's personal style and can have a significant effect on his or her mood and sense of well-being. Poet Maya Angelou cut to the heart of what a home can do for a person when she said, "The ache for home lives in all of us, the safe place where we can go as we are and not be questioned."[30]

Many American ideas about home design and furnishings can be traced back to colonial days. The earliest homes were rudimentary, often just one room without windows, as glass was difficult to obtain. As people accumulated wealth, they added windows and divided their space into more than one room. Scholar Ann Smart Martin traces the history of how Americans furnished these homes.[31] Young couples setting up households in the early eighteenth century typically purchased pots and pans, sheets and blankets, and tables and chairs. Those who could afford more would acquire candlesticks, additional linens, and silver. "A mirror or dressing table, a bookcase or chest of drawers, were the first of many household furnishings that began to elaborate and define wealth and allow greater storage and attention to fashion. Increasingly, goods also had specialized functions and hierarchically segmented spaces," Martin says.[32] By the mid-eighteenth century, settlers were purchasing china and cutlery for serving tea and more elaborate meals. This early period set the stage for Americans to focus their attention on filling their homes not just with the bare necessities but with luxury goods. It also raised an issue that is still relevant today: how to balance function with a desire for display and status.

No matter what the time period, a bright, comfortable, well-arranged interior space can reinforce the primal sense of comfort and safety that Angelou identified. Chief among the considerations is a home's access to natural light. In *A Pattern Language*, a classic guide to architecture and planning, authors Christopher Alexander, Sara Ishikawa, and Murray Silverstein state, "Modern buildings are often shaped with no concern for natural light— they depend almost entirely on artificial light. But buildings which displace natural light as the major source of illumination are not fit places to spend the day."[33] Even for those who spend a great deal of time indoors, daylight is important as a reference point because it helps maintain the body's circadian rhythms. *A Pattern Language* recommends that homes be designed with two windows in each room, preferably facing in different directions. "The fact is that very few things have as much effect on the feeling inside a room as the sun shining into it," say the authors.

Those who suffer from seasonal affective disorder find that a sun-filled home can help them cope. Remember LaDonna Bates? She recalls a "marvelous" experience near a sunny window when she was about eight years old and a snowstorm had kept her home from school. "To this day," LaDonna says, "if I have trouble going to sleep, I go back and think about that day."

Even a small room can be arranged to maximize sun and natural light. When at home, my patient Gloria likes to sit at a glass desk that faces a large window through which she can look out over the Charles River in Boston. Her bright, Caribbean-inspired decor helps her feel warm and happy, and a large mirror next to the window adds even more light. A vase of sunflowers on the coffee table brightens up the space.

The authors of *A Pattern Language* also talk about how rooms can help make the transition between outdoors and indoors, so there is not an abrupt change from a vestibule or covered porch right into a living space. That's why wealthy Victorians created homes with different rooms for different purposes: the entranceway for arrival; the parlor for conversation; the dining room for meals; and a dark, cramped kitchen for cooking to be done by servants. Nowadays, a mudroom is a popular way to create a kind of transitional space, with a place for coats, boots, and perhaps a bench to make it easy to don or shed our outdoor garments.

Once the living space itself is designed or set up, choosing what to put in a home can be overwhelming, given the vast array of furniture choices and housewares. Interior designer Betsy Bassett of Newton, Massachusetts, believes most people have a home-decorating style, even if they have not yet articulated it. "How you surround yourself with things is what defines you. You may be unconscious of this, but what you bring into your house is what you think will give you peace and pleasure," she says.[34]

People who are able to tap into their own sense of aesthetics are the most likely to create an environment that feels comfortable. What works for one person may not work for another. Bold turquoises and oranges might energize one person, while someone else would feel overwhelmed by this palette and prefer subdued earth tones. One person may want nothing whatsoever on the tabletops, while another might want to display all her books and knickknacks from travels because she enjoys the memories they bring.

No matter what, the challenge for any home dweller is to find a way to create a sense of harmony out of the whole living space, even if it is small. A different scheme in each room makes the home look "disjointed," Bassett says. "You want a color and a theme that connects from room to room, that links you visually as you move through the house." For example, artwork on the wall in the dining room could echo the colors on the pillows in the adjacent living room.

Creating a more harmonious living environment need not require the skills of a decorator or the *Extreme Makeover: Home Edition* team. Small changes, keeping within an individual's aesthetics and budget, can add up to a big psychological boost. Furniture can be moved to maximize natural light or create a smooth traffic flow from room to room. A small addition, such as a house plant or a colorful doormat, could help ease an unpleasant transition from outdoors to indoors. Repainting a wall works wonders, too. "A can of paint is almost like a restart button. It's very therapeutic," says Bassett.

Tending to Yourself

As I've listened to my patients' stories and worked with them to resolve their emotional hotspots, I have come to recognize the important role that environmental factors play in determining their emotional state. This is something that I have experienced personally as well. But my main passion—and, of course, my area of expertise—is in helping people work through their internal emotional struggles.

It can be relatively easy to plant a garden or to arrange the rooms and things in your house to help you feel as comfortable and at ease with your life as possible, but how do you go about the difficult challenge of tending to yourself? How do you lay out a strategy for achieving adaptive control over your emotional calendar? Remember that adaptive control is the ability to bend flexibly with the winds of change—to prepare for and respond positively to the emotional hotspots in our calendars. Adaptive control is a learning process and something that we all struggle with, especially when confronted with new or particularly painful hotspots. I would love to say that reading this book will be enough, but mastering your emotional calendar is not something that comes overnight. It takes time, patience, experimentation, and persistence.

Adaptive control is about choice. I like to use the analogy of a car. Sometimes we feel as though we are passengers in life, watching the car drive down scenic passes, through murky tunnels, and across treacherous, icy paths. Sometimes we feel as though that car is skidding out of control. We cling white-knuckled to the door handle, screaming at the driver to slow down, speed up, or don't miss that left turn.

This is not how most of us would prefer to proceed along the road of life. To avoid that sense of impending catastrophe, we need to put ourselves in the driver's seat. Once there, we must accept the possibility that each of us can, in fact, drive the vehicle. And then, like the good drivers that we all can be, we set off. We must expect that there will be dangerous spots and tricky stretches of road and that when they appear we can respond calmly and thoughtfully to them.

Just as there are various techniques we can use to improve our driving, there are methods and tools that we can use to help us deal with our emotional hotspots, such as the ones we've already discussed: turning off the autopilot, taking our emotional pulse, and using positive awareness strategies. And the good news is, no one has to go it alone.

PUTTING YOURSELF IN THE DRIVER'S SEAT

Gaining awareness of your patterns and developing greater mindfulness in daily life can give you a sense of perspective that will allow you to achieve adaptive control over your life.

One of my patients found success in applying these techniques. Her significant issues with distractibility and inattentiveness had limited her ability to attend college. She felt particularly vulnerable in October, when her distractibility tended to reach a peak. Anticipating this problem, she came up with a plan that would help her persevere. Knowing her tendency to procrastinate, she kept organized and worked toward obtainable daily goals. She resolved not to accept excuses for falling behind in her work. For extra help, she signed up for on-campus academic and organizational coaching. These measures made her feel like she was getting into the driver's seat instead of going along for the ride.

COPING: THREE STRATEGIES

Once you have put yourself into the driver's seat, there are three strategies you can use to help yourself use mature adaptations to respond to situations in positive ways. These are all forms of adaptive control.

The first strategy is utilizing *emotional distance* to maintain stability. This is not the same as avoidance or denial, neurotic defenses that can have unintended long-term consequences. I like to talk with patients about "titrating" their emotional distances, which means carefully measuring your avoidance to keep from getting overwhelmed. Strategically managing your encounters with challenging coworkers and reducing your level of commitment to a stressful project are examples of ways you can confront sources of conflict without being overwhelmed by them.

The second strategy you can use is to *change your external circumstances*. This is an approach that Susan Folkman, an expert on coping at the University of California at Berkeley, refers to as "problem-focused coping." Problem-focused coping is simply "addressing the problem that causes distress." Problem-focused coping might include making a plan of action or concentrating on the future.[35]

Many people make a particular effort to travel during hotspots in their emotional calendar, removing themselves from the weather that brings them physical or mental discomfort. But changing your external circumstances can be much simpler than that. Even something as straightforward as drinking ice water on a hot day can help to alleviate your physical and emotional discomfort. As Rachel became accustomed to her outdoor lifestyle, for example, she took a problem-focused approach by going shopping. "My first weekend off, I went out and I bought a good raincoat, waterproof boots, and polypropylene clothing," she says. By eliminating the physical discomfort caused by the cold and rain, she reduced its emotional weight. All that remained was the memory of discomfort, the persistent idea that winter should be sad, that wind should be scary, and that rain should be miserable.

Dealing with these memories requires the third strategy: *changing your attitude*, or what is known as "emotion-focused coping."[36] Emotion-focused coping refers to behavior that is aimed at "ameliorating the negative emotions associated with the problem." Helpful emotion-focused coping behaviors can include engaging in distracting activities and seeking emotional support.[37] Emma reads her children's books and Steve flies his model airplanes. Even watching a movie or listening to music can be helpful.

One participant on an Internet message board wrote, "I live in Houston. As the fall comes to an end, I get increasingly frustrated at how consistently hot and sunny it is. I am in *desperate* need of some books describing verdant hills or cloudy, dreary skies or a snowy seacoast—basically any sort of books that have that sort of atmosphere."[38]

And of course sometimes visiting a psychiatrist can help.

Rachel went on a summer canoe trip that was plagued by blackflies, swarming insects that feed on blood and leave stinging welts behind. At the height of her physical discomfort, she was sitting on a rock on the bank of the river when she spotted a dragonfly nymph in the process of metamorphosis. The insect's transformation, she said, became a symbol for her need to transcend and transform apparently negative experiences into more positive ones (dragonflies eat blackflies). At the same time, it served as a reminder of the importance of stopping and appreciating the moments of beauty, expected or unexpected, that fall on everyone's emotional calendar.

Begin to identify the influence that your emotional calendar has on your daily life. Mindfulness therapy—a combination of meditation and other practices—can train you to filter the various influences on your behavior and recognize which of your emotions come from external sources, such as emotional cues and seasonal triggers.[39]

BECOMING AWARE: TAKE IT IN STAGES

Adaptive control is an ongoing process. Once you've identified the various causes of your emotional upheaval, it can take a long time, as well as a lot of work, to employ an appropriate coping strategy to the point that it alleviates your emotional hotspot. It involves taking your emotional pulse on a regular basis, not just when you feel that you are about to collapse under the weight of your anxiety. And it means putting yourself in the driver's seat in a number of ways and in different situations over time.

Case in point: me. The summer following Sally's late visit to Nantucket, I was amazed to find myself falling back into the state of agitation that descended toward the end of August. I could feel myself becoming anxious. I was initially caught by surprise, as if this had never happened before. But, simply by becoming aware of my emotional state, I was able to reflect on it and understand that it was "that time of year again." This allowed me to step back and think about how I wanted to respond. I did not want to fall prey to the same old pattern, so I worked to change my reactions to what was happening and—most impor- tant—to what was going to happen.

I wondered if I could think of that period not as a torture to be endured but as a special time, a transition period from mostly pleasure to mostly work, a blend of family togetherness and pro- fessional preparation. Could I deliberately use the time to get a mental jump on the work waiting for me in the fall, rather than forcing myself to try to relax (but failing miserably) during the last days of August? What if I set aside just an hour or two a day during which I would review my plans for the year, read a scholarly article, correspond with colleagues, or start jotting down some thoughts for a lecture I would be giving in Novem- ber? I would be flexible about when the hour came, so I could be with my wife or my kids when they wanted to be with me. And what if I explicitly let my family know that I had identified this hotspot on my emotional calendar, that it was a challenge for me—in fact, had been the cause of my crankiness during Sally's last visit—and that this was my way of dealing with it?

The strategy worked. The following year (you see, these things take some time!), as the last two weeks of August approached, I recognized the signs of my anxiety much earlier and more clearly than ever before. I informed my family that the "cranky time" was upon me. (Their response, in essence, was "Duh.") One day, after lunch, when everybody else was lying on the beach or resting, I retreated to a little nook and did nothing more than take out all the papers that I had stuffed in my briefcase before I left for vacation and sort through them. It was a good start. I felt much better at the end of the hour. By the time Labor Day rolled around, I was ready to jump into the fall routine. I can't say that my strategy has transformed the end of August into my favorite time of year, but I will say that I have come to appreciate this interesting mixture of work and play, of unstructured family time and professional focus.

BRIAN: MAKING DRASTIC CHANGES TO HIS EXTERNAL CIRCUMSTANCES

My patient Brian, the ex–band manager, became quite expert at employing our coping strategies to improve his outlook. You'll remember that Brian is an alcoholic in recovery who now struggles with overeating. Winter is a particularly difficult time for him, in part because of the increased alcohol and food consumption around him at holiday parties. When he was managing that famous rock band, Brian was responsible for booking gigs around the world. In its early days, he would book the band into off-season venues, such as Scandinavia in the winter, and this contributed to his depression. As Brian became more aware of his sensitivities, however, he started to book as many concerts as he could in tropical climates during the winter. This allowed him to keep himself busy during the time when he was most vulnerable, and in a climate that was healthier for his state of mind; it also removed the immediate temptation of going to holiday parties with friends and family where alcohol—and food—would be flowing freely.

You can develop this form of emotional distance through a guided imagination exercise. Imagine you are facing a familiar temptation. You recognize not one but two paths ahead. You choose to resist the temptation, and you reward yourself for this with congratulations and a reward. Like Brian, you treat your avoidance of harm to yourself as a cause for celebration. You feel stronger and more purposeful. Brian came to see that resisting overeating was a sign of his own strength, an affirmation of his determination to live a healthy life. The key factors enabling this change are evident: support and understanding, some creative thinking, trust, openness to trying something other than the same old way, determination, and honest appraisal, all repeated over and over.

Brian also took a more drastic step in changing his external circumstances. In order to distance himself from his old life and to ensure that he saw his family only on certain, prearranged occasions, he moved from New England to the Southwest. Brian loves his family, but he finds it difficult to stay in control in their company, particularly in the winter. "There are a lot of alcoholics in my family, and Christmas always triggers that," he explains. "My alcoholism would get out of control. It's not that my family is horrible, but seeing them triggers the memories. So now I see them individually. I don't see them all together at Christmas."

He had been thinking about leaving Boston for a long time before he finally felt ready to take that step. His main concern, as it turned out, was that moving might feel like running away from his problems. But as he came to understand (and as I tried to help him see), there is a difference between running away and changing your circumstances. Brian's alcoholism is under control, and he is much better able to manage his tendency toward overeating than when we first started working together. But every time he returned to Boston from a trip, the temptation to return to these old vices was as strong as ever. No matter how carefully he timed the trip, or how well he took care of himself, the return to his home environment remained a trigger. For Brian, the best solution, though a diffi-cult one, was to remove himself from that situation entirely.

Medicating: Some Prescriptions

We often turn to antibiotics to cure infections, such as taking penicillin for strep throat. Another group of medications helps relieve the mental and emotional distress that can be triggered by a number of factors, including our seasonal emotional dis-ruptions. In instances when the stress takes on a physical com-ponent, such as the urge to sleep all day, medication can be a reasonable choice. I have discussed many other strategies that can help you cope with seasonal changes, but medication is an important modality of care—just one, but certainly one that should not be overlooked.

We self-medicate all the time, using relatively low doses of both stimulants and sedatives to adjust our energy levels, often on a daily basis. Coffee and beer, green tea and yoga, chocolate and aerobic exercise are all different pairs of "uppers" and "down-ers," which, for many of us, are a part of everyday life. If you are considering taking medication to help you better manage your hotspots, start by making a list of what you already do to regu-late your energy level. Do you drink coffee several times a day or just in the morning? Do you pour a glass of wine to help yourself relax after a long day at work? Consider the effects you are trying to achieve, and then investigate what is medically available.

Over-the-counter medications, "natural" supplements, and traditional herbs are plentiful and often promise relief of stress, anxiety, and fatigue. Go to the supermarket, health food store, or pharmacy and look at the shelves. This will give you an idea of the range of products that address emotional issues. Take an informal survey of what's available, and then plan to come back after you have done more research. Consult the person behind the counter, ask a friend with a similar problem, or go to a credible Internet source of health information. A health care provider (trained in Eastern or Western medicine) who is trustworthy and knowledgeable in the area that you are seeking can also advise you. Just understand that you are not likely to find a miracle cure-all no matter what you do. There is a lot of unreliable information and uncertainty about how and why over-the-counter medications or supplements work. Each person's reaction to a particular medication can vary greatly, and interactions between medications can be dangerous. The best thing to do is inform yourself thoroughly so that you are comfortable with your decision. You may find good results. I'm a believer in taking what works.

Call a doctor when you feel you need professional advice and treatment. A general practitioner or internist has training and experience in common psychological issues and, if needed, can write a prescription. Let your doctor be your partner in determining your health care needs. A psychiatrist is the medical specialist most likely to be an expert in the integration of psychotherapeutics, psychopharmacology, and brain science. You can ask for a consultation with a psychiatrist much the same way as you ask to see another medical specialist. I can vouch for Western prescription medications, which, judiciously applied, can bring great relief to people who are experiencing excessive suffering and despair.

FOR ANXIETY

There is a relationship between anxiety and performance. As anxiety goes up, performance goes up—for a time. Anxiety actually motivates us positively, improving our performance. Then it plateaus. After that, more anxiety just gets in the way and impairs our performance. When anxiety is excessive, we benefit from something that reduces the feelings that interfere with our ability to think clearly, respond adaptively, and perform as required. So when you can't reduce anxiety enough by using mindfulness and coping strategies, when your anxiety is interfering with your ability to function, when your feelings of anxiety seem to have a life of their own and are out of proportion to what is happening to you, then some form of medication may indeed be indicated.

For the short-term relief of anxiety from an understandable cause or circumstance (such as the threatened loss of a job), I might recommend minor tranquilizers to a patient. First, however, I'd have to review the patient's physical well-being and current medications to make sure that there is no existing medical cause of the suffering. Then I'd want to screen for other psychiatric conditions, most notably major depression, which could present similarly. Minor tranquilizers are mainly in the benzodiazepine class, for example diazepam (Valium), clonazepam (Klonopin), lorazepam (Ativan), oxazepam (Serax), and alprazolam (Xanax). In low doses as needed, or on a standing basis for a week or two, these medications can reduce anxiety so that people can function better. The goal is to improve the patient's ability to utilize the broader range of coping tools more effectively again.

Of course, there can be problems. Contrary to having the desired effect, benzodiazepines can cause a vulnerable individual to become psychologically or even physically dependent on their effects. Instead of fostering a renewed and strengthened ability to cope, this class of medication can lure a person into doing less and less and relying on the medication more and more. People with known susceptibilities to alcohol abuse or dependency should probably not take benzodiazepines at all, or perhaps very cautiously under very close monitoring. If someone is taking a medication in this class and seems to need more and more, or seems slowed down or otherwise impaired, then it is time to evaluate if the medication is useful or simply compounding the situation. An honest and careful look at the entire picture—the patient's circumstances, the reaction to these circumstances, coping strategies, medications, and substance use or abuse—should yield an answer about whether it is wise to use a benzodiazepine.

Often the old-fashioned advice of moderation makes the most sense. Just as too much sleep or too much exercise can be a problem, so can too much reliance on any one way of coping, including a medication in the benzodiazepine class. Still, in certain cases, a little can go a long way toward helping someone improve his or her self-reliance and versatility in handling difficult circumstances.

FOR DEPRESSION

As is the case with anxiety, if the full extent of a patient's suffering cannot be easily or fully explained by circumstances— if there seems to be a separate, additional element contributing to a patient's distress—it's time to explore further. I look into the family and personal history to try to determine any vulnerability to an anxiety disorder or to depression. These are medical illnesses, not faults of character or failures of coping. Yet these illnesses can cause a person to feel inadequate in face of a challenge, even simply getting through the day. Anxiety disorders and depressive disorders have lives of their own, a quality that needs special attention to treat. Medications are often part of a comprehensive treatment plan and might include a wide variety of antidepressants—there are twenty-seven in America at this point—such as sertraline (Zoloft), escitalopram (Lexapro), bupropion (Wellbutrin), duloxetine (Cymbalta), and others.

Antidepressant medication must be taken under a doctor's supervision, and it is important for patients to know what to expect. They do not work right away. It may take two or three weeks to notice any benefit. Interestingly, someone else in the patient's life may be the first to see the glimmer of a response, often in the form of increased energy or improved sleep or appetite. Most people who are going to realize a full treatment response in six months will see a little something in the first several weeks, especially when others point it out. But their subjective state—actually feeling better—may take the longest to improve.

Not all of the initial side effects of antidepressants are desirable. Sometimes antidepressants can cause fatigue, alterations in sleep, gastrointestinal disturbance, or decreased sexual functioning. The longer view is that such side effects are reversible, likely to be relatively minor, and may subside by themselves with a little bit of time. After about six to eight weeks, the patient and doctor can take stock of the emotional benefits and the lingering side effects, and then weigh one against the other. For almost everybody, the effects of depression are far worse than the side effects of antidepressants!

FOR BIPOLAR DISORDER

Another fairly common problem, often seasonally related, is the occurrence or worsening of bipolar disorder. To put it more technically, the seasons can exacerbate a recurrence of a person's underlying vulnerability to a bipolar spectrum disorder. Just as we all have a normal variation in our moods, persons with bipolar disorder have amplified mood swings that get completely out of control. A manic state—elevated, expansive, irritable moods coupled with racing thoughts, impulsivity, impaired insight and judgment, and decreased need for sleep lasting for weeks at a time—is extremely dangerous. The onset may be spontaneous, stress related, or seasonally triggered. Indeed, it is very common for patients with bipolar disorder to need an adjustment in their medication come spring and fall.

The signs that someone is going into a manic episode can be dramatic, and the person may even seem happy about it. Or he or she may seem irritable all the time or find everyone else irritating, have racing thoughts, and no longer need to sleep much at night. In this situation, there is an urgent need for treatment, which is best left to an expert. Dosing down incoming stimulation by encouraging rest and relaxation, adherence to a healthy schedule, and good sleep habits is critical. A helpful kind of basic therapy called "interpersonal and social rhythm therapy" incorporates these elements into a treatment protocol, in which medication is critically important. "Minor" tranquilizers such as the benzodiazepines, as well as "major" tranquilizers in the atypical antipsychotic family such as quetiapine (Seroquel), aripiprazole (Abilify), and olanzapine (Zyprexa) can work quickly over hours and days to provide initial stabilization. Individuals with bipolar disorder will come to want to be protected against these kinds of episodes by staying with a mood-stabilizing medication for the long term.

It is entirely natural to adjust the treatment according to the season of the year. We are all stimulated by the effects of the seasons, and someone with bipolar disorder feels these effects, too, perhaps more so. An adjustment in medication can help level out the effects of a seasonal change.

KNOWING WHEN TO SEEK HELP

Most of us understand that we become physically worn down during periods of stress, making us more vulnerable to catching a cold or the flu. What we may not realize is that our emotional immunity can also get run down, making it easier for a major depression to develop. This would be an understandable—but not necessarily expected—consequence of prolonged stress.

Just as you would seek out the best medical advice possible—either from your family doctor or from a specialist—were you to develop an infection, so, too, would you be best cared for by seeking expert medical opinion in instances when you are really overwhelmed. The goal is not to be medicated but rather to relieve unwarranted suffering, taking what proves to be effective only as long as necessary. For instance, antidepressants are not prescribed indefinitely. A patient is expected to take the medication or medication combination that has worked to treat the depression for approximately six months to two years before tapering off. The idea is to try to ensure that the risk of relapse is minimized.

Whether your mood is triggered by seasons or something else, if you find that you are unable to function normally, please don't hesitate to contact a psychiatrist. Many forms of help, including medications, are available, and you need not suffer alone.

Elizabeth: Developing a Method for Managing the Calendar

The story of how Elizabeth, one of my patients, became aware of her hotspots and found a way to better manage her emotional calendar demonstrates how the process can work. Elizabeth is a person with whom I worked for several years; I have built on her story to bring in some relevant issues that other patients contend with but that were not contained in Elizabeth's narrative.

At thirty-eight, Elizabeth had a good marriage and two fine kids, a nine-year-old girl and a six-year-old boy. She was a lawyer and had recently returned to work full-time in her suburban town at a small firm that specialized in environmental law. Elizabeth was a petite woman, very smart, and a little tightly wired. Although she could be incredibly perceptive about the emotional and psychological issues affecting her family members and her clients, she was surprisingly less sensitive to her own emotional states, especially as they related to the seasons.

Elizabeth and I had been working together for some years. She was prone to anxiety and had experienced two bouts of depression, one when she left her job with a high-powered law firm in the city and another after her second child was born. This particular year, though stabilized on antidepressant medication, Elizabeth's anxiety increased markedly in early fall. We discussed it, and she talked about the new pressures of her job, the difficulties of juggling work and family responsibilities, her worries about her son's school, and her sense that she had very little time for herself anymore. I sensed something more behind her anxiety, however, and at last we identified it. She was suffering from that cultural seasonality that, as we've seen, is so common to many Americans: Thanksgiving foreboding.

As much as we love this most American of holidays, it can also be one of the most intense times of the year, combining large doses of time spent with family members whom we may have "issues" with, political overtones connected with the election period just passed, deep memories of childhood Thanksgivings, and the marking of the inescapable transition from late fall to early winter.

This particular year, Elizabeth and her husband would be hosts to a combined Thanksgiving of Elizabeth's extended family as well as her husband's relatives. She expected twenty-nine people, many of whom she had not seen for years. "Just managing the preparation of the meal is stressful enough," she said. "Who's going to bring which dishes? Who has special dietary requirements? What can we cook ahead of time? Are we going to serve wine, even though Uncle Jack is on the wagon? Who's going to sit where?"

Hosting a large dinner party can certainly be stressful, but I knew that Elizabeth was a very capable woman who could pull off that part of the holiday. But by early November, Elizabeth was in a state of anxiety more pronounced than I had ever witnessed with her. At last, after much discussion, she began to talk about the hotspots and triggers of her personal calendar. "This goes all the way back to my senior year in college," she said, her mind obviously wandering back to those times, almost two decades earlier. "This is the first time that I've had a similar kind of Thanksgiving event, with relatives from both my mother's and father's side of the family. My mother's clan is a pretty liberal bunch, all very high-energy and extremely opinionated. My father's family is more conservative and reserved, but with equally strong opinions. Just to complicate matters, that year I brought home a new guy I had been dating for several months. Jay was smart and clever, but could also be a bit of a wiseass. We were talking about getting married."

Things did not go at all well. The boyfriend drank too much wine at dinner. The discussion turned political, and Elizabeth's father lost his temper and asked Jay to leave the table. Jay stormed out of the house. Elizabeth stayed behind but was angry at her father all evening and through the next day. Jay and Elizabeth broke up soon after the holiday. She blamed her father for destroying the relationship, but they never really talked about it. They had been tense together around the Thanksgiving holiday ever since.

No wonder Elizabeth was having trouble with the approaching Thanksgiving. What to do? We talked about her options. Could she avoid the situation? Not really. She wanted to see her relatives, or most of them anyway. And she had agreed to host the dinner and she was a woman who kept her promises.

"But are there certain aspects of the holiday you can avoid?" I asked.

"I suppose so," said Elizabeth. "I could just ban political topics."

"What about your attitude?" I asked. "Is there another way to think about that long-ago Thanksgiving? Was it really so bad? Was the talk of marriage really serious?"

"No," she said. And then a smile crossed her face. "I was already having my doubts about Jay, and that episode made it clear that we were not right for each other. I pretended to be mad at my father, but I was actually pleased that it happened. And I guess I've been a bit mad at myself that I've never told Dad that."

I'm happy to report that Elizabeth managed her Thanksgiving very differently that year. She delegated most of her tasks. She avoided discussion of politics. And she even had a conversation with her father about the fateful senior-year Thanksgiving. He revealed that he had been worried about her, not mad at all, and had been attuned to her concerns about her career moves and her relationship with Jay.

Her success in managing Thanksgiving proved helpful to Elizabeth at other times of the year when she felt an emotional disruption. She learned to recognize when she was feeling out of sorts and began to engage in a dialogue with herself.

Wait a minute, she would say to herself, something's going on that isn't normal. I don't feel exactly right, and I need to do something to manage this condition. I want to feel different than I do. She would then consider the seasonal effects:

Is there a physical or environmental factor that's having an effect on my mood?

Is there a cultural seasonality that's influencing me?

Is there some personal hotspot that's burning a hole in my mind?

By talking with herself, making an inventory of the seasonal issues, and then thinking about various ways to change her situation—creating emotional distance, changing external circumstances, or adjusting her attitude—Elizabeth can now enjoy, in particular, her favorite holiday more than she has in years and also finds, in general, a new sense of ease and enjoyment in the passing of the seasons.

13

Seasonal Embrace

Live each season as it passes; breathe the air, drink the
drink, taste the fruit, and resign yourself to the
influences of each.

—HENRY DAVID THOREAU, *Journal*, August 23, 1853

MANY YEARS AGO, my father told me about how he had learned to deal with the onset of winter when he was a student in college. He and his friends made a pact: when the first snow of the year began to fall, they would stop whatever they were doing (even if it meant excusing themselves, ever so politely of course, from class), gather their friends, and meet at Ferdinand's, their favorite (now closed) restaurant and pub in Harvard Square for food, drink, and time together. My father remembered one of these get-togethers with particular fondness, because that year the first snow appeared at 11 A.M. and they spent the whole day and much of the night socializing. Their ritual continued beyond their college careers. Just thinking of it, I get a smile at my first sighting of snow to this day.

I think of my father's practice as a good example of *seasonal embrace*. Seasonal embrace means becoming well attuned to your own reactions to life—conveniently divided up into organized, manageable time periods: the seasons. It allows you to recognize how you have been conditioned to feel and what you have come to expect from different periods of the year, so that you can change your life for the better: do more of what's working, do less of what's not, and adopt new strategies to fill in or substitute as needed.

Taking good care of yourself as you deal with your seasonal hotspots involves many simple, everyday activities you can engage in to help maintain your physical and emotional homeostasis. Some bits of advice are simple: Keep a regular schedule. Plan ahead. Sleep well. Watch your diet. Exercise. Work your mind. Practice self-relaxation. Listen to music. Pay attention to grooming. Visit your doctor and dentist regularly. If needed, take medications faithfully and at the proper times and dosages. Get good support from the right people. When you need help with any seasonal emotional disruption, be willing to seek support and gain perspective from others.

As we've seen, many people who feel anxiety about the effects of the seasons will keep it to themselves. They bottle it up and choose not to talk with anyone about it. As a result, they worry even more, and their anxiety heightens still further. Then they feel ashamed of their feelings. To make matters worse, they often judge themselves harshly, feeling ashamed of their shame. Many people will isolate themselves during such intense times. This tendency to isolate is in itself an action that usually prolongs the anxiety and results in even more reactive behavior that, although it is intended to preserve homeostasis, is actually harmful. Seeking support from other people may be stressful at first, but it ultimately reduces one's anxiety. It's important to learn how to select the right people: those who can be most helpful and supportive and offer strength and companionship.

As you step back and take a look at your emotional calendar, you may at first feel daunted. You may see a year loaded with emotional hotspots that you dread. Yet your ultimate goal should be to find the joy that each season has to offer—even the ones that used to create trouble for you. Making these adaptations in your outlook and your response can be energizing and fun.

Embracing each of the seasons may mean paying closer attention to nature and the cycling seasons or even renaming them to fit your own emotional calendar. I love, for example, the ways of the Massa people, who have a specific name for each of their seasons—including the "merry season" and the season for "strolling and visiting," although we'd probably want to avoid their "fattening season"! Such close observation of nature takes the emotional bite out of each season and gives everyone in that community a reason to appreciate what's going on around them. Perhaps you could find your own ways to anticipate and mark each season according to the small but profound changes in nature that you can observe around you.

Looking Back, Looking Forward

Let me close as I began, with a story from my own life, because it illustrates how our hotspots can wax and wane and how the emotional calendar constantly shifts and evolves as we move forward with our lives.

About two years ago, I felt we needed to sell our cottage by the shore on Nantucket, for many reasons. There had once been a line of cottages that stood between us and the ocean. Then along came the "perfect storm" of 1991, which caused an enormous surge of tide that washed away that entire stretch of houses. In the years that followed, I watched the sea inch closer to our cottage and I began to fear that we would suffer the same fate. My concerns were validated by an erosion study that predicted eventual doom for our easternmost island coastline. Every fall, as the hurricanes blew northward from the Caribbean, I lost night after night of sleep, worrying that another "big one" would cause our beloved property to be washed away. What's more, we were finding less and less time to spend on the island. The girls had other summer pursuits. My wife and I were traveling back and forth to Los Angeles. We finally came to the conclusion that a period of our lives was coming to an end, and it was time to sell. We did so reluctantly and a bit tearfully.

I don't get to spend as much time on the ocean as I once did, which is perhaps ironic considering that I am bicoastal now, with one practice on the East Coast and the other on the West. Even so, my emotional calendar, come summer and fall, remains deeply affected by hotspots related to those summers, marked with countless triggers. My family feels them, too. Only I, however, seem to suffer the restiveness of summer's end. I still feel I have to *get going* while my wife and daughters enjoy their lingering.

But as I become more used to tracking and honoring my own emotional calendar, I find that I can cycle through the years more smoothly and with more confidence. I hope you can, too. Gradually, you can banish the dread of sad anniversaries and bad stretches of emotional weather. In its place will be strategies for taking care of yourself during these times and finding the beauty even in the gray slush of winter or the wilting heat of summer. You can learn to make the most of the seasonal times that you already enjoy, such as a birthday or an exhilarating return to an outdoor sport after a year away from it. Each month will become filled, not just with appointments and obligations, but with times to enjoy and embrace, leading to your own beautiful journey through the year.

Notes

~

1. The Emotional Calendar

1. Alison Lester, *The Journey Home* (Boston: Houghton-Mifflin, 1991).
2. Ashley Eckes and Heidi Liss Radunovich, "Trauma and Adolescents," University of Florida IFAS Extension, October 2007, http://edis.ifas.ufl.edu/pdffiles/FY/FY100400.pdf.
3. "Statistics," National Institute of Mental Health, http://www.nimh.nih.gov/health/topics/statistics/index.shtml.
4. David S. Goldstein and Irvin J. Kopin, "Evolution of Concepts of Stress," *Stress* 10, no. 2 (2007): 109–20.
5. Louis J. Battan, *Weather in Your Life* (San Francisco: W. H. Freeman, 1983).
6. "Seasonality of Youth's First-Time Use of Marijuana, Cigarettes, or Alcohol," *NSDUH Report*, June 4, 2004, http://oas.samhsa.gov/2k4/season/season.htm.
7. Neeru Gupta, "Seasonality of Premarital First Intercourse Among Brazilian Youth," *Electronic Journal of Human Sexuality* 10 (December 3, 2007), http://www.ejhs.org/volume10/seasonality.htm.
8. Wilpen Gorr, Andreas Olligschlaeger, and Yvonne Thompson, "Short-term Forecasting of Crime," *International Journal of Forecasting* (June 13, 2000): 586.
9. Kevin Drum, "Everything in Its Season," CBS News, September 4, 2007, http://www.cbsnews.com/stories/2007/09/04/politics/animal/main3233732.shtml.
10. George J. Dudycha and Martha M. Dudycha, "Some Factors and Characteristics of Childhood Memories," *Child Development* 4, no. 3 (September 1933): 265–78.
11. Goldstein and Kopin, "Evolution of Concepts of Stress," 109–20.
12. B. Headey and A. Wearing, "Personality, Life Events, and Subjective Well-Being: Toward a Dynamic Equilibrium Model," *Journal of Personality and Social Psychology* 57, no. 4 (1989): 731–39.

13. M. Davern, R. Cummins, and M. Stokes, "Subjective Wellbeing as an Affective-Cognitive Construct," *Journal of Happiness Studies* 8, no. 4 (December 2007): 429–49.

14. Goldstein and Kopin, "Evolution of Concepts of Stress," 109.

15. David H. Uttal, "Maintaining Homeostasis Is Certainly Important, but Can It Lead to Change?" *PsycCritiques* 36, no. 12 (1989): 1054–55.

16. L. Lu, "Understanding Happiness: A Look into the Chinese Folk Psychology," *Journal of Happiness Studies* 2 (2001): 416.

17. Ibid., 416–17.

18. George D. Freier, *Weather Proverbs: How 600 Proverbs, Sayings and Poems Accurately Explain Our Weather* (Tucson: Fisher Books, 1992), 96.

Opening Section to Part I

1. "Indigenous Weather Knowledge," Australian Government Bureau of Meteorology, http://www.bom.gov.au/iwk/.

2. The Intergovernmental Panel on Climate Change, "Summary for Policy Makers," *Climate Change 2007: Synthesis Report*, www.ipcc.ch/publica tions_and_data/ar4/syr/en/spm.html.

3. Danielle Scott, "The Impact of Climate Change on Golf Participation in the Greater Toronto Area (GTA): A Case Study," *Journal of Leisure Research* (June 22, 2006): 363.

4. Tracee Hamilton, "Endless Sports Seasons," *Washington Post*, December 20, 2009.

5. Ibid.

6. Judy Battista, "Craving for Football Drives a Season Without End," *New York Times*, May 3, 2009.

7. Bill Carter, "A Television Season That Lasts All Year," *New York Times*, September 23, 2008.

2. Supercharged Summer

1. Interview with Jane Rupley.

2. Shirley A. Morrissey et al., "Seasonal Affective Disorder: Some Epidemiological Findings from a Tropical Climate," *Australian and New Zealand Journal of Psychiatry* 30, no. 5 (1996): 579–86.

3. Interview with Dr. Shirley Morrissey.

4. Ibid.

5. Gupta, "Seasonality of Premarital First Intercourse."

6. Julie Henry and Roya Nikkhah, "Welcome to Casual Sex-on-Sea," *Sunday Telegraph*, August 1, 2004.

7. "Two Out of Three Small Business Owners Planning Summer Break, According to the Open Small Business Network 2004 Semi-Annual Monitor from American Express," PR Newswire, May 19, 2005.

3. The Reality of Fall

1. U.S. Census Bureau, April 27, 2009, http://www.census.gov/.

2. "2010 General Hunting Season Dates," New Hampshire Fish and Game Department, http://www.wildlife.state.nh.us/Hunting/hunting_dates_and _seasons.htm.

3. Rod Davis, "Autumn Awakenings," *Virginia Hunting Today*, December 12, 2007, http://virginiahuntingtoday.com/blog/index.php/2007/12/12/autumn-awakenings/.
4. Ibid.
5. "Sports Addiction," Professor's House, http://www.professorshouse.com/family/health/sports-addiction.aspx.
6. "Super Bowl XLIV Most Watched Super Bowl of All Time," Nielsen Company, February 8, 2010, http://blog.nielsen.com/nielsenwire/media_entertainment/super-bowl-xliv-most-watched-super-bowl-of-all-time/.

4. The Wide Hand of Winter

1. Readers' Comments, "Brought on by Darkness, Disorder Needs Light," *New York Times*, December 18, 2007, http://community.nytimes.com/article/comments/2007/12/18/health/18mind.html.
2. Randy J. Nelson and Gregory E. Demas, "Seasonal Changes in Immune Function," *Quarterly Review of Biology* 71, no. 4 (December 1996): 511–48.
3. Michael Tougias, *The Blizzard of '78* (Yarmouth Port, MA: On Cape Publications, 2003), 101–2.
4. Rosalyn Simons, comment, "The Blizzard of '78 Website," http://hullnantasket.homestead.com/Blizzardof78hull.html.
5. Ibid.
6. Harold Crapo, comment, "Blizzard of '78 Letters," http://archive.southcoasttoday.com/daily/02-03/02-02-03/f05lo214.htm.
7. Gloria Proulx-Morrissette, comment, "Blizzard of '78 Letters," http://archive.southcoasttoday.com/daily/02-03/02-02-03/f05lo214.htm.
8. Peter J. Howe, "The Class of '78," *Boston Globe*, February 6, 2008, http://www.boston.com/news/local/articles/2008/02/06/the_class_of_78/.
9. Kim Moore, comment, "The Blizzard of '78 Website," http://hullnantasket.homestead.com/Blizzardof78hull.html.
10. Marie Smiley Wright, comment, "The Blizzard of '78 Website," http://hullnantasket.homestead.com/blizzardof78nonhull.html.
11. "Mardi Gras," The History Channel, http://www.history.com/topics/mardi-gras/.

5. Spring: What *Do* You Want?

1. *Chun Feng Chen Zui De Ye Wan (Spring Fever)*, Cannes Film Festival, http://www.festival-cannes.com/en/archives/ficheFilm/id/10901155.html.
2. Alfred Jay Bollett, *Plagues and Poxes: The Rise of Epidemic Disease*, quoted in Michael Kesterton, "Social Studies: A Daily Miscellany of Information," *Globe and Mail*, February 20, 2008.
3. C. Nicholson, "Does 'Spring Fever' Exist?" *Scientific American* 298, no. 4 (April 2008): 116.
4. Ellen Ketterson and Melissa-Ann Scotti, "Sex Ends as Seasons Shift and Kisspeptin Levels Plummet," *Science Daily*, December 29, 2006, http://www.sciencedaily.com.
5. Natalie Angier, "Seasons Sway Human Birth Rates," *New York Times*, October 2, 1990, http://www.nytimes.com/1990/10/02/science/seasons-sway-human-birth-rates.html.

6. Elena Conis, "Why the Spring Makes Us Feverish," *Los Angeles Times*, March 31, 2008.

7. Nicholson, "Does 'Spring Fever' Exist?" 116.

8. Michele A. Berdy, "Spring Weather Brings Spring Illnesses," *Moscow Times*, April 25, 2008.

9. Ibid.

10. Howard Gabennesch, "When Promises Fail: A Theory of Temporal Fluctuations in Suicide," *Social Forces* 67, no. 1 (1988): 138.

11. Ibid.

12. Jennifer Forbes, "Allergies and Mental Health," *Mental Health Minutes*, August 22, 2007, http://jenniferforbes.blogspot.com/2007/08/allergies-and -mental-health.html.

13. Paul S. Marshall, Ph.D., Christine O'Hara, R.N., and Paul Steinberg, M.D., "Effects of Seasonal Allergic Rhinitis on Fatigue Levels and Mood," *Psychosomatic Medicine* 64 (2002): 684–91, http://psychosomaticmedicine .org/cgi/content/full/64/4/684.

14. Terri Mauro, "Spring Fever: Welcome to Silly Season," *Parent Connection* 14, no. 4 (Spring 2009).

15. Ibid.

16. Andrew Raven, "Body Clock out of Whack," *Straits Times* (Singapore), April 20, 2008.

17. Ibid.

6. Running Hot and Cold

1. "A Frosty Take on All Things 'Cold,'" *All Things Considered*, August 25, 2009, http://www.npr.org/templates/story/story.php?storyId=112211478.

2. "Animals in Winter," Connecticut Audubon Society, http://www.ctaudubon .org/conserv/nature/animals.htm.

3. "Species Pages: *Rana sylvatica*," The Virtual Nature Trail at Penn State New Kensington, http://www.psu.edu/dept/nkbiology/naturetrail/species pages/woodfrog.htm.

4. Latanya Odden, "You at 50 Below," *Extreme Alaska: Surviving the Cold Rush*, http://www.uaf.edu/journal/extreme/surviving/Feeling_the_Pinch/50 _below.html.

5. Bill Streever, *Cold: Adventures in the World's Frozen Places* (New York: Little, Brown and Co., 2009), 44–45.

6. Ibid., 123.

7. Scott Freeman, *Biological Science* (Upper Saddle River, NJ: Prentice Hall, 2002), 740.

8. Vasoconstriction is a very real phenomenon that can cause significant discomfort. Raynaud's syndrome, for example, is a condition in which the blood vessels in the hands and feet narrow in response to even mild drops in temperature. Fingers turn ghostly white and go numb enough that it's hard for people to complete simple tasks. When it gets warmer and blood starts to flow again, the fingers sting and can turn bluish-purple in color.

9. "'Wrap Up' Advice to Stop Colds," CNN Health, November 14, 2005, http:// www.cnn.com/2005/HEALTH/11/14/cold.chill/index.html.

10. Tara Parker-Pope, "11 Health Myths That May Surprise You," *New York Times*, June 29, 2009, http://well.blogs.nytimes.com/2009/06/29/11-health-myths-that-may-surprise-you/.
11. Matt Sloane, "Recognizing Symptoms of Hypothermia," Blog: Paging Dr. Gupta, December 18, 2006, http://www.cnn.com/HEALTH/blogs/paging.dr.gupta/2006/12/recognizing-symptoms-of-hypothermia.html.
12. "Frozen Woman: A 'Walking Miracle,'" CBS News, 2000, http://www.cbsnews.com/stories/2000/02/03/broadcasts/main156476.shtml.
13. Count Philippe-Paul de Ségur, *Napoleon's Russian Campaign*, trans. J. David Townsend (Santa Barbara, CA: Greenwood Press, 1976), 73.
14. Keith Suter, "Snow and Ice Defeat Would-Be Conquerors," *Daily Telegraph*, January 24, 2006.
15. Ségur, *Defeat*, 83.
16. Vasodilation is what makes your face red when you exercise.
17. Arnold G. Nelson, "Body Cooling and Response to Heat: A Commentary," *Wilderness and Environmental Medicine* 12, no. 1 (March 2001): 32–34.
18. Ibid.
19. "I Will Survive," *Outside*, September 2004, http://outside.away.com/outside/features/200409/top_survival_stories_8.html.
20. "Dehydration," MERCK Online Medical Library, http://www.merck.com/mmhe/sec12/ch158/ch158b.html.
21. Samantha Booth, "Do You Feel Washed Out?" *Daily Record*, July 4, 2007.

7. Living in Light and Dark

1. Urmila Parlikar, "Seasonal Affective Disorder: Blame It on Sunlight and Serotonin," Swedish Medical Center, http://patton.lexipal.com/article/29035.
2. Fiona Proffitt, "How Flowers Know It's Spring," *Science Now*, February 13, 2004.
3. T. J. Nicholls, A. R. Goldsmith, and A. Dawson, "Photorefractoriness in Birds and Comparison with Mammals," *Physiological Reviews* 68 (January 1988): 133–71.
4. "Vitamin D: A Bright Spot in Nutrition Research," *Harvard Heart Letter*, December 2009, 3.
5. Ibid.
6. Kenneth P. Wright Jr. et al., "Caffeine and Light Effects on Nighttime Melatonin and Temperature Levels in Sleep-Deprived Humans," *Brain Research* (July 22, 1997): 82.
7. M. Mila Macchi and Jeffrey N. Bruce, "Human Pineal Physiology and Functional Significance of Melatonin," *Frontiers in Neuroendocrinology* 25 (September–December 2004): 178–79, 182.
8. Nicholson, "Does 'Spring Fever' Exist?" 116.
9. Nigel Hawkes, "Daylight Is Key to Good Night's Sleep for Babies . . . and Parents," *Times* (London), November 23, 2004.
10. Kathryn Moynihan Ramsey and Joseph Bass, "Obeying the Clock Yields Benefits for the Metabolism," *Proceedings of the National Academy of Sciences of the United States of America* 106 (March 17, 2009): 4069–70.

11. Macchi and Bruce, "Human Pineal Physiology," 178–79.
12. Pat Thomas, *Under the Weather: How the Weather and Climate Affect Our Health* (London: Fusion Press, 2005), 30.
13. Anahad O'Connor, "Daylight Saving Time Can Affect Your Health," *New York Times*, March 10, 2009.
14. Jane Gordon, "Bill in Favor of Sunlight Won't See the Light of Day," *New York Times*, February 13, 2005.
15. Julia Preston, "Daylight Savings, the Worst of Times," *New York Times*, April 3, 1999.
16. Ibid.
17. Macchi and Bruce, "Human Pineal Physiology," 185.
18. Mary Emma Allen, "Sundowning in Mother's Alzheimer's Life," *Alzheimer's Notes*, October 4, 2008.
19. Karin Sparring Björkstén, Peter Bjerregaard, and Daniel F. Kripke, "Suicides in the Midnight Sun," *Psychiatry Research* 133 (February 28, 2005): 211.
20. Leo Sher, "Cortisol and Seasonal Changes in Mood and Behavior," *Psychiatric Times* (October 1, 2006).
21. Jean Malaurie, *The Last Kings of Thule: With the Polar Eskimos, As They Face Their Destiny*, trans. Adrienne Foulke (New York: Dutton, 1982), 80.
22. Lyle Dick, "'Pibloktoq' (Arctic Hysteria): A Construction of European-Inuit Relations?" *Arctic Anthropology* 32 (1999): 1–42.
23. Bruce Henderson, *True North: Peary, Cook, and the Race to the Pole* (New York: W. W. Norton & Co., 2005), 125–26.
24. Lawrence A. Palinkas and Peter Suedfeld, "Psychological Effects of Polar Expeditions," *Lancet* 371 (2008): 154.
25. Alan Miller, "Epidemiology, Etiology, and Natural Treatment of Seasonal Affective Disorder," *Alternative Medicine Review* 10, no. 1 (2007): 5.
26. Asa Westrin and Raymond W. Lam, "Long-Term and Preventative Treatment for Seasonal Affective Disorder," *CNS Drugs* 21, no. 11 (2007): 902.
27. Miller, "Epidemiology, Etiology," 6.
28. Ibid., 6–7.
29. Interview with LaDonna Bates.
30. Macchi and Bruce, "Human Pineal Physiology," 178–79.
31. Parlikar, "Seasonal Affective Disorder."
32. Macchi and Bruce, "Human Pineal Physiology," 178–79.
33. Tammie R. Smith, "Light Pollution: Star Chasing," *National Geographic* (November 2008), http://ngm.nationalgeographic.com/2008/11/light-pollution/follow-up-text.
34. Malaurie, *Last Kings of Thule*, 223.
35. Gretel Ehrlich, *The Future of Ice: A Journey into Cold* (New York: Pantheon Books, 2004), xiii.
36. *The Arctic* (Oakland, CA: Lonely Planet Publications, 1999), 367–69.
37. Sarfraz Manzoor, "The Lights Are Out—Let's Party," *The Observer*, January 11, 2009, http://www.guardian.co.uk/travel/2009/jan/11/tromso-norway-arctic-winter-travel?page=1.

38. Anne Berit, e-mail to the research team, December 1, 2009, http://statistik knett.no/.
39. Manzoor, "The Lights Are Out—Let's Party."

8. Wind and Storm: The Weather of Catastrophe

1. Mark de Villiers, *Windswept: The Story of Wind and Weather* (New York: Walker, 2006), 74.
2. Lyall Watson, *Heaven's Breath: A Natural History of the Wind* (London: Holder and Stoughton, 1984), 339–41.
3. Thomas Mann, *Death in Venice*, trans. Martin C. Doege, http://www.scribd .com/doc/985179/Death-in-Venice.
4. Ibid.
5. E. Ahmbach et al., "Fatal Myocardial Infarction and Tyrolean Winds (the Foehn)," *Lancet* 339, no. 8805 (May 30, 1992): 1362–63.
6. L. J. Cooke, M. S. Rose, and W. J. Becker, "Chinook Winds and Migraine Headache," *Neurology* 54, no. 2 (2002): 302.
7. Ibid.
8. Jan deBlieu, *Wind: How the Flow of Air Has Shaped Life, Myth, and the Land* (Boston: Houghton-Mifflin, 1998), 183–84.
9. Philip Eden, "Days of Toxic Darkness; Britain's Weather: The Great London Smog of 1952," *Daily Telegraph*, November 30, 2002.
10. Paul Simons, "Foggy, Smoggy Days," *Times* (London), November 30, 2002.
11. Charles Dickens, *Our Mutual Friend* (London: Chapman and Hall, 1907), 398.
12. Simons, "Foggy, Smoggy Days."
13. James Moore, "I Was There: Great Smog, 1952," *Mirror*, December 15, 1999.
14. "A Proper Pea-Souper—The Terrible London Smog of 1952," Nickel in the Machine, http://www.nickelinthemachine.com/2008/11/a<->proper-pea -souper-the-terrible-london-smog-of-1952/.
15. Ibid.
16. Richard Baldwin, "The Great London Smog of 1952," *Economist*, August 20, 2008, http://www.economist.com/blogs/freeexchange/2008/08/the_great_ london_smog_of_1952.
17. Booth, "Do You Feel Washed Out?"
18. Ibid.
19. Thomas, *Under the Weather*.
20. Ibid.
21. Interview with Susan Mortweet VanScoyoc.
22. Jane E. Brody, "After the Hurricanes, the Inner Storm for Children," *New York Times*, September 27, 2005.
23. Ibid.
24. National Institute of Mental Health, "What Are the Symptoms of PTSD?" National Institutes of Health, January 21, 2009, http://www.nimh.nih.gov/ health/publications/post-traumatic-stress-disorder-ptsd/what-are-the -symptoms-of-ptsd.shtml.

25. Ann Hackmann et al., "Characteristics and Content of Intrusive Memories in PTSD and Their Changes with Treatment," *Journal of Traumatic Stress* 17 (June 2004): 232.
26. Anke Ehlers et al., "The Nature of Intrusive Memories After Trauma: The Warning Signal Hypothesis," *Behaviour Research & Therapy* 40 (September 2002): 999–1002.
27. The Intergovernmental Panel on Climate Change, "Summary for Policymakers," *Climate Change 2007: Synthesis Report*, http://www.ipcc.ch/pdf/assessment-report/ar4/syr/ar4_syr_spm.pdf.
28. Shirley A. Morrissey and Joseph P. Reser, "Natural Disasters, Climate Change and Mental Health Considerations for Rural Australia," *Australian Journal of Rural Health* 15 (2007): 121–22.
29. Garrison Keillor, "The News from Lake Wobegon," *A Prairie Home Companion*, June 7, 2008.
30. Graham Brink, "Blowing Our Minds," *St. Petersburg Times*, December 3, 2006.

9. Emotional Memory

1. Judy Foreman, "Do People Urinate More During the Cold Months?" *Boston Globe*, December 22, 2008, http://www.boston.com/news/health/articles/2008/12/22/do_people_urinate_more_during_the_cold_months/.
2. Daniel Schacter, *Searching for Memory: The Brain, the Mind, and the Past* (New York: Basic Books, 1996), 163–79.
3. Ibid.
4. Ibid.
5. Endel Tulving, "Episodic Memory: From Mind to Brain," *Annual Review of Psychology* 53 (2002): 1.
6. Ibid., 5.
7. George E. Vaillant, "Vaillant's Glossary of Defenses," in *Ego Mechanisms of Defense: A Guide for Clinicians and Researchers* (Washington, DC: American Psychiatric Press, 1992), 246–47.
8. F. Scott Fitzgerald, *The Great Gatsby* (Oxford: Oxford University Press, 1998), 144.
9. Robert Andrews, *The Columbia Dictionary of Quotations* (New York: Columbia University Press, 1993), 6.

10. The Cultural Calendar

1. Igor de Garine, "Culture, Seasons and Stress in Two African Cultures," in *Seasonality and Human Ecology: 35th Symposium Volume of the Society for the Study of Human Biology*, ed. S. J. Ulijaszek and S. S. Strickland (Cambridge: Cambridge University Press, 1993), 197.
2. E. Beaglehole, "Emotional Release in a Polynesian Community," *Journal of Abnormal and Social Psychology* 32 (1937).
3. Stuart Jeffries, "Alistair McGowan: 'Football Cost Me My Partner, Ronnie Ancona,'" *Guardian*, September 23, 2009, http://www.guardian.co.uk/tv-and-radio/2009/sep/23/alistair-mcgowan-obsession-with-football.
4. "Synopsis: *A Matter of Life or Death: Or How to Wean a Man Off Football*,"

https://www.waterstones.com/waterstonesweb/products/ronnie+ancona/
alistair+mcgowan/a+matter+of+life+and+death/6734912/.
5. Hunter S. Thompson, "Don't You Dare Cancel Football," ESPN.com, http://
sports.espn.go.com/espn/page2/story?page=thompson/040727.
6. James Sullivan, "Hunter S. Thompson Dies," *Rolling Stone*, February 21,
2005, http://www.rollingstone.com/.
7. Douglas Brinkley, "Football Season Is Over," *Rolling Stone*, September 8,
2005, http://www.rollingstone.com/.
8. Tom Chivers, "Bah Humbug: The 10 Worst Things About Christmas," *Telegraph*, December 18, 2009.
9. Ibid.
10. "Holidays & Occasions," Hallmark, http://corporate.hallmark.com/Holiday.

11. Your Personal Calendar
1. "Can You Give Me a Sad Birthday Quote?" Yahoo! Answers, May 2009,
http://ph.answers.yahoo.com/question/index?gid=20090514063747AAL1Ts9.
2. Deane, "No One Is Coming to My Daughter's Birthday Party," Baby Crowd
Online Forums, April 12, 2006, http://www.babycrowd.com/forums/birth
day_party/No_one_is_coming_to_my_daughter_s_birthday_party__
pg114489472480/.
3. Tilly, "I'm Sad Because My Birthday Is Coming Up," Yahoo! Answers, November 2009, http://answers.yahoo.com/question/index?qid=20091116183328AAH
kQZG.
4. Bashō, "First Day of Spring," in *Visions from Earth: A Book of Gentle Wisdom*, ed. James R. Miller (Bloomington, IN: Trafford Publishing, 2004), 35.

12. Looking Outward, Looking Inward
1. Vaillant, "Vaillant's Glossary of Defenses," 243–52.
2. Joshua Wolf Shenk, "What Makes Us Happy?" *Atlantic*, June 2009, http://
www.theatlantic.com/doc/200906/happiness.
3. Red Earth Farms, http://www.redearthfarms.org/.
4. Red Earth Farms Member Bios, http://www.redearthfarms.org/alyson.html.
5. Gordon H. Orians, "Nature & Human Nature," *Dædalus* (Spring 2008): 46.
6. Ibid.
7. International Community for Ecopsychology, http://www.ecopsychology.org/.
8. Martin Jordan, "Back to Nature," *Therapy Today* 20 (April 2009): 26–28.
9. Michael Pollan, *Second Nature: A Gardener's Education* (New York: Atlantic Monthly Press, 1991), 3–4.
10. Daniel Defoe, *Robinson Crusoe* (New York: Cosmopolitan Book Corporation, 1920), 83.
11. Ibid., 137.
12. I. Söderback, M. Söderström, and E. Schälander, "Horticultural Therapy:
The 'Healing Garden' and Gardening Rehabilitation Measures at Danderyd Hospital Rehabilitation Clinic, Sweden," *Pediatric Rehabilitation* 7,
no. 4 (2004): 245–60.
13. Ruth Page, *Ruth Page's Gardening Journal* (Boston: Houghton Mifflin,
1989), 29.

14. C. Milligan, A. Gatrell, A. Bingley, "Cultivating Health: Therapeutic Landscapes and Older People in Northern England," *Social Science & Medicine* 58, no. 9 (May 2004): 1782.

15. Ibid., 1787.

16. Ibid., 1790.

17. Interview with Jane Rupley.

18. Page, *Ruth Page's Gardening Journal*, 126.

19. Carol Olwell, *Gardening from the Heart: Why Gardeners Garden* (Berkeley: Antelope Island Press, 1990), 60.

20. Pollan, *Second Nature*, 205.

21. George Washington's Mount Vernon Estate & Gardens, http://www.mount vernon.org/.

22. Vince Staten, *Can You Trust a Tomato in January? Everything You Wanted to Know (and a Few Things You Didn't) About Food in the Grocery Store* (New York: Simon & Schuster, 1993), 16–17.

23. Slow Food USA, http://www.slowfoodusa.org/.

24. Ibid.

25. Chefs Collaborative, http://chefscollaborative.org/.

26. Barbara Kingsolver, *Animal, Vegetable, Miracle: A Year of Food Life* (New York: HarperCollins, 2008), 3.

27. Ibid., 316.

28. Gaining Ground, *The Gaining Ground Table* (Concord, MA: Gaining Ground, 2009).

29. Wendell Berry, *The Gift of Good Land: Further Essays, Cultural and Agricultural* (San Francisco: North Point Press, 1982), 168.

30. Maya Angelou, *All God's Children Need Traveling Shoes* (New York: Random House, 1986), 11.

31. Ann Smart Martin, "Makers, Buyers, and Users," *Winterthur Portfolio* 28, no. 2–3 (Summer–Autumn 1993): 141–57.

32. Ibid.

33. Christopher Alexander, Sara Ishikawa, and Murray Silverstein, *A Pattern Language: Towns, Buildings, Construction* (New York: Oxford University Press, 1977), 108.

34. Interview with Betsy Bassett.

35. Susan Folkman and Judith Tedlie Muskowitz, "Coping: Pitfalls and Promise," *Annual Review of Psychology* 55 (2004): 751.

36. Ibid.

37. Ibid.

38. "Please Recommend Books with Lush/Sunless Scenery," Internet Movie Database, Board: Books, November 16, 2009, http://www.imdb.com/board/bd0000052/threads/.

39. Ellen J. Langer, *Mindfulness* (Reading, MA: Addison-Wesley Pub. Co., 1989).

Acknowledgments

How can I acknowledge and thank the many kind, hardworking, and supportive spirits that have helped to make this book possible? With pleasure, and one at a time, I suppose.

I am grateful to my wife, Elline, and to my daughters, Ashley and Else, for their love, tremendous inspiration, and for never dispiriting me in this effort. I owe countless thanks to my mother, Helen, for all her devotions and for always believing in me (despite my occasional resistance to her sage advice!), to my cousins—Jim, Anne, Jane—who are so much like brother and sisters to me, and to my aunt Caroline and uncle David. My eternal thanks, too, to my dad, who with my mother, put me on the path to receiving an excellent education, from primary school through medical school. I am grateful to the many teachers and professors who guided me along the way and to those who became close friends, especially my roommates at Harvard and, of course, James Hwa Chou.

I'd like to thank all of the people who shared their seasonal travails for this book, and most especially my patients, who agreed to share their innermost lives with me and the members of my research team. Those who were my patients, and those who were not were equally honest, candid, and articulate about their experiences and insights. Their stories and what we learned from them are at the heart of this book, and I couldn't have written it without them. I must acknowledge, too, the subject-matter experts who provided incredibly helpful materials and comments. I am grateful as well for the loyal support of my home Department of Psychiatry at the Beth-Israel Deaconess Medical Center, Harvard Medical School.

A thousand thanks to my natty friend and collaborator John Butman, of Idea Platforms, Inc., and his wonderful team of researchers and writers. John's talent for developing ideas and structuring chapters helped give the book its shape, and his skill with a pen helped me convey my true voice in print. The IPI team included project coordinator Janine Liberty, writer/researchers Anna Weiss and Hannah Alpert-Abrams, and administrative associate Louisa Slocum. They worked closely with independent contributors Barbara Lynn-Davis and Clara Silverstein, and the team had early editorial counsel from Martine Bellen. Their efforts were indispensable.

My sincere gratitude to my literary agent, Todd Shuster of Zachary Shuster Harmsworth, whose enthusiasm for this book, as well as his insightful comments, were instrumental in its construction. In addition to helping me get the proposal to where it needed to be, Todd also gracefully shepherded me around the New York publishing world, securing the loyal interest of my publisher, Paul Golob at Times Books. My editors at Times Books—Robin Dennis, Dedi Felman, Annetta

Hanna, and Serena Jones—provided invaluable comments and corrections and brought the manuscript into its final form. And, many thanks to my publicist, and new friend, Valerie Allen in L.A.

Cheers!

Index

About the Author

JOHN R. SHARP, M.D., is a psychiatrist and neuropsychiatrist who serves on the medical staff at the
Beth Israel Deaconess Medical Center in Boston. He
is on the faculty at Harvard Medical School and at
the David Geffen School of Medicine at UCLA, and
he divides his time between Boston and Los Angeles.